*Edited by*
*Randall Hinshaw*

# World Recovery without Inflation?

*The Johns Hopkins*
*University Press*
*Baltimore and London*

The Johns Hopkins University
  Press
701 West 40th Street
Baltimore, Maryland 21211

The Johns Hopkins Press Ltd,
  London

*Library of Congress Cataloging in
Publication Data*

Main entry under title:
World recovery without inflation?

Edited transcript of a conference
entitled "Proposals for global
economic recovery," held May 1983
and sponsored by the Bologna Center,
the Claremont Graduate School, and
the Hamburg Institute of Economic
Research.
  Includes indexes.
  1. Fiscal policy—Congresses.  2.
Inflation (Finance)—Congresses.  I.
Hinshaw, Randall Weston.  II. Johns
Hopkins University. Bologna
Center.  III. Claremont Graduate
School.  IV. HWWA-Institut für
Wirtschaftsforschung-Hamburg.
HG63.W66 1985    338.9    85-188
ISBN 0-8018-2764-7 (alk. paper)

*To the Memory of*  **Lionel Robbins**
*1898–1984*

# Contents

# Acknowledgments

Any list of acknowledgments for a project requiring as many months of preparation as the 1983 Bologna conference is bound to be incomplete, and is likely to involve serious sins of omission. In the hope that I have minimized such sins, I would like to express the following words of deep appreciation.

First of all, abundant thanks are due to the conference members, who interrupted busy schedules in order to spend two demanding days in northern Italy. In particular, I would like to thank Richard N. Cooper, who superbly combined the traditional roles of chairman and moderator, roles that earlier had been played with consummate skill by Willard L. Thorp and the late Lord Robbins.

But the conference would not have been possible without generous financial support. Because of the world recession—which inspired the conference theme—funds were much more difficult to raise than usual, and it was necessary to approach a larger than usual number of sources. Major matching grants were obtained from the Italian central bank (Banca d'Italia) and the Hamburg Institute of Economic Research, with badly needed additional funds provided by S. G. Warburg & Co. Ltd., Getty Oil Company, the Bank of America, and Union Bank. The two memorable evening banquets, which took place at gastronomically famous Bologna restaurants, were hosted and paid for by Italian commercial banks—the first by the Banco di Roma and the second by the Banca Commerciale Italiana.

Institutions provide funds, however, only when persuaded to do so by their top officials. Among such individuals, all of whom at various times have been members of the "Bologna-Claremont" dialogues, I would particularly like to thank Giovanni Magnifico, Economic Counsellor to the Banca d'Italia; Armin Gutowski, President of the Hamburg Institute of Economic Research; Lord Roll of Ipsden, Chairman of S. G. Warburg & Co. Ltd.; H. Robert Heller, Vice President for International Economics of the Bank of America; J. Howard Craven, Senior Vice President and Economist of Union Bank;

and Romeo dalla Chiesa, President of the Banco di Roma. I would also like to thank Henry C. Londean, Corporate Public Affairs Manager of Getty Oil Company, who arranged the grant from that institution. As president of one of the three academic cosponsors of the 1983 meeting, Dr. Gutowski devoted innumerable hours to conference planning, and, as always, his enthusiasm, good humor, and wisdom made him a great joy to work with.

Under the able leadership of Robert G. Gard, the officers and staff of the Johns Hopkins Bologna Center were of immense help in staging the conference. Among the officials, I would particularly like to name Frederick D. Olessi, Assistant Director; Hannelore Aragno, Registrar; R. William Schwab, Bursar; and Neilita Landau, Alumni Affairs Director; and, among the staff, Angelo Buldini, Paola Dabbous, Antonio Poltroniere, and Germana Rinaldi. Of the Bologna Center faculty, I am greatly indebted to Professor Stefano Zamagni for invaluable assistance in getting in touch with Italian commercial banks and to Professor John Harper for helpful counsel and warm support. I also owe much to my exceedingly able student assistants, Jennifer Lewis and Ron Lissak, who helped me surmount many a minor—and more than one major—crisis.

Finally, I cannot end this list without acknowledging my perpetual debt to my wife, Pearl, who, as always, was of enormous help in conference matters, and to our son Frederic, who, interrupting his vacation, arrived in Bologna a few days before the meeting and, with characteristic energy and initiative, plunged into the last-minute preparations, some of which involved hard physical labor. In countless ways, his rich experience backstage at earlier conferences was of immense assistance in preventing the operation of Murphy's Law.

# Contributors

Sven W. Arndt, Professor of Economics, University of California, Santa Cruz

Giorgio Basevi, Professor of Economics, University of Bologna

Richard N. Cooper (Chairman), Maurits C. Boas Professor of International Economics, Harvard University; Undersecretary of State for Economic Affairs, 1977–81

W. M. Corden, Professor of Economics, Australian National University

J. Howard Craven, Senior Vice President and Economist, Union Bank

Otmar Emminger, President, Deutsche Bundesbank, 1977–79

Armin Gutowski, President, Hamburg Institute of Economic Research

H. Robert Heller, Vice President for International Economics, Bank of America

Randall Hinshaw, Distinguished Visiting Professor of Economics, The Johns Hopkins University Bologna Center

Conrad C. Jamison, Vice President and Economist, Security Pacific National Bank (retired)

Lord Kaldor, Fellow, King's College, Cambridge University, Special Adviser to the Chancellor of the Exchequer, 1956–75

Giovanni Magnifico, The Economic Counsellor, Banca d'Italia

Heinrich Matthes, Director, Deutsche Bundesbank

J. E. Meade, Cambridge University; Nobel Laureate in Economics

Robert A. Mundell, Professor of Economics, Columbia University

Giuseppe Pennisi, Director General, Office of Public Investment Evaluation, Ministry of the Budget, Rome

Gisele Podbielski, Senior Associate Member, St. Anthony's College, Oxford University

Hans-Eckart Scharrer, Director, Department of Monetary Affairs, Hamburg Institute of Economic Research

Jürgen Schröder, Professor of Economics, University of Mannheim

*Robert Triffin*, Université Catholique de Louvain; Frederick William Beinecke Professor of Economics Emeritus, Yale University

*Roland Vaubel*, Kiel Institute of World Economics

# World Recovery without Inflation?

Randall Hinshaw

# The Third Bologna Dialogue: Background

Surrounded by several dozen rapt student observers at the Johns Hopkins University Bologna Center, a small group of leading economists met in May 1983 for a two-day dialogue on global economic recovery—more precisely, on the perplexing problem of how to achieve a lasting situation of high employment without a renewal of serious inflation. Planned during the worst months of the recent world recession, the meeting was jointly sponsored by the Bologna Center, the Claremont Graduate School, and the Hamburg Institute of Economic Research. It was the ninth in a series of biennial dialogues that had originated in Bologna in 1967; of the earlier meetings, four had taken place in Europe—two in Italy, two in Germany—and four in Claremont, California. This book is an edited transcript of the 1983 tape recording.

As at the earlier conferences, great effort was made to select a theme that would permit participants to talk about issues of foremost current concern. The rather bland wording of the 1983 theme, "Proposals for Global Economic Recovery," was intended to be broad enough to include both domestic and international matters and to embrace at least the Western world, including the so-called Third World. The plural wording of "Proposals" was deliberate, mainly because there was little or no prospect of agreement on a single program. Disagreement among economists is proverbial, and, in order to obtain a wide range of viewpoints, this tendency was consciously exploited in choosing the participants.

Such a procedure has been questioned by some activists, who feel that a conference should produce a report consisting of policy recommendations supported by a majority of the membership. But that way of doing things was rejected from the very beginning of the series. The late Lord Robbins, who served so splendidly as moderator of the dialogues until his illness in 1982, made it clear at the outset that he would never be placed in a position where he might feel impelled to proclaim to the world why, on given policy recommendations, he disagreed with the majority. The wise stand that he took has made it possible over the years to attract economists of the highest distinction for frank and penetrating dialogues in a friendly and often exciting atmosphere—"electric" was the word used by a faculty observer of the 1983 meeting. The success of the format can be judged by the longevity of the series; certainly, it would never have been possible to continue the series for so many years if the participants had considered the exercise a waste of time.

Partly because of the smaller than usual number of participants—a product of the recession!—and partly because of the skill of Richard Cooper, who combined the traditional roles of chairman and moderator, the 1983 dialogue was particularly lively. There were no prepared papers, and Chairman Cooper guided the proceedings with a light rein; he aptly described the conferences, in several of which he had participated, as "intellectual free-for-alls." The discussion in Bologna included more than the usual amount of good-humored banter; except for the laughter none of this has been eliminated in the editing.

Professor Cooper made it clear at the first session that he would interpret the wording of the conference theme as broadly as possible to include longer-run as well as short-run issues, Third World problems, and issues in the international terrain—in particular, trade policy, exchange-rate policy, and, as a concession to Robert Mundell, the question of whether gold should be restored as the anchor of the international monetary system.*

The inclusion of longer-run issues was eminently justified. The first signs of recovery were already in evidence when the 1983 meeting took place, but the key question was how to get back to a high level of economic activity without a return to the inflation that had plagued the 1970s. Indeed, it had been the widespread concern about accelerating inflation that had led to the recession in the United States and Western Europe. Max Corden, a highly articulate participant, repeated the charge that the recession was deliberately manufactured in an effort to reduce inflation; in his view, it was the result of a conscious move along the famous Phillips Curve, the curve that traces the "trade-off" between inflation and unemployment. Viewed as an anti-inflationary measure, the recession was certainly success-

---

*The role of gold in the international monetary system was the theme of the first Bologna conference in 1967. The dialogue is reproduced in *Monetary Reform and the Price of Gold: Alternative Approaches*, ed. Randall Hinshaw (Baltimore: Johns Hopkins Press, 1967).

ful; inflation was dramatically brought down from double-digit levels. But the cost was great in the form of unemployment, which in the United States reached a peak in December 1982 of 10.8 percent of the civilian working force—the highest figure since the Great Depression.

Of course, if the Phillips Curve were a fixed entity of the traditionally assumed shape, measures to reduce unemployment would automatically increase the rate of inflation. Thus the central issue of the conference, expressed in this language, was how to change the shape, or, as Professor Mundell put it, how to shift the position, of the Phillips Curve. From this perspective, the question addressed by the conference was of much broader interest and significance than the specific problem of how to get out of the deepest recession since World War II. Indeed, it was the question that in one way or another had occupied the attention of all the conferences in the series since the second Bologna dialogue of 1971. At that meeting, Robert Mundell made the rather startling proposal of using fiscal policy and monetary policy in opposite directions: expansionary fiscal policy, in the form of tax cuts, to achieve high employment and monetary restraint to achieve price-level stability.* Thus Bologna became the cradle, if not the birthplace, of latter-day "supply-side economics."† The Mundell prescription attracted wide attention, and profoundly affected the policies of the Reagan administration.

But the world of April 1971 was very different from the world of May 1983. In the earlier period, interest rates were low, oil was $1.65 a barrel, the U.S. budget for the preceding calendar year was $11.4 billion, exchange rates were pegged, and the dollar was still anchored to gold. By 1983, all these conditions had radically changed, and, with the exception of the drastic increase in the price of oil, about which little could—or perhaps should—be done, all the changes were strongly criticized by one or more of the conference participants.

It would be presumptuous and unfair to attempt a summary of the 1983 dialogue; the opinions with all their qualifications, are best expressed by the participants themselves. Suffice it to say that there was sharp disagreement on fiscal policy, on monetary policy, on the need for international coordination of economic policies, and on how

---

*Professor Mundell's statement of his position is reproduced in the 1971 conference volume, *Inflation as a Global Problem*, ed. Randall Hinshaw (Baltimore: Johns Hopkins University Press, 1972), chap. 8.

†The adjective "latter-day" is used advisedly, because nineteenth-century classical economics strongly emphasized the supply side.

best to deal with the critical problem of Third World debt. At the same time, most if not all of the participants were worried about the exploding U.S. budget deficit and its effect on interest rates; high interest rates were regarded by all as a major obstacle to a lasting recovery. And no one at the conference appeared happy about the decade of experience with flexible exchange rates, though there was complete lack of agreement on remedies.

But no one expected easy solutions. The atmosphere at the Bologna meeting was one of disenchantment—disenchantment with monetarism of the doctrinaire variety, with Keynesian economics in a 1983 context, with the rosier versions of supply-side economics, with "rational expectations," and, as already noted, with floating exchange rates. At the opening session, Professor Gutowski well expressed the general mood of disillusionment when he declared that even the proponents of such approaches appear to have lost their faith in them. Commenting on this statement with approval, Robert Mundell said it showed "that economics is beginning to grow up a bit—to get out of its diapers if not out of its rompers. We have to start thinking again, and that's a happy thing for all of us."

And so it is. If the ensuing dialogue helps to stimulate this process of rethinking, it will have amply served its purpose.

Lord Kaldor
Otmar Emminger
Giovanni Magnifico
Armin Gutowski
Robert Triffin
Robert A. Mundell

# Issues in Recovery: Six Perspectives

*Chairman Richard N. Cooper:* Let me begin by saying something about how we plan to dispose of the next two days. The wording of our theme, "Proposals for Global Economic Recovery," is deliberately extremely general to allow us to range as far as we want to range— and, given the composition of our group, are likely to range—but I interpret it to include the present global macroeconomic situation, exchange-rate arrangements, reserve-generation arrangements, the acute foreign-debt problem of some of the developing countries, and (unavoidably, since Bob Mundell is with us) the highly controversial subject of gold. I think we shall find ourselves inevitably being drawn into issues of trade policy to some extent. It is certainly not my intention to try to organize the conference by subject matter, but I have no doubt that we shall touch on all these topics. If, in fact, one or another of them somehow drops out of sight, I shall feel free to introduce it.

This is the ninth in our series of conferences, which began back in the mid-1960s. The meetings have been intellectual free-for-alls. No formal papers are presented. In that respect, our procedure differs from the normal kind of academic conference, but we have prevailed upon several of you to make opening remarks of ten minutes or so just to get things going.

One of the problems with this kind of conference is to allow everyone a fair opportunity but at the same time permit continuity in the discussion. To try to straddle that dilemma, we will adopt the now familiar "Machlup convention," whereby anyone can interrupt the normal order by raising both hands, provided he confines his remarks to the topic immediately at hand. If he has other remarks of a more general nature or on a different topic, then he has to go back to his position on the list. We all make our living by talking, but there are twenty-four of us, and that doesn't give a lot of time for each individual during the next couple of days. I hope, therefore, that you will all respect the other participants, confine your remarks to the highest priority items, and not abuse the two-handed intervention technique.

Unless there are questions about our procedure or about our overall schedule, I propose to start with my list, which already has on it Lord Kaldor, Dr. Emminger, Giovanni Magnifico, Armin Gutowski, Robert Triffin, and Robert Mundell. Nicky [Lord Kaldor], do you want to lead off?

*Lord Kaldor*: I didn't expect to be the first to be called on, but I regard it as a great honor. Our topic, global economic recovery, is of foremost importance and one that exercises the minds of economists and ministers of finance over most of the developed world. And I think there are certain propositions which are proved so often that they should be accepted as uncontroversial.

One such proposition is that it is very difficult for governments to promote economic recovery without an international coordination of economic policies. This international coordination should include agreement on the nature and timing of the economic stimuli which governments wish to introduce. In addition, governments ought to agree—as they came close to agreeing in the famous Bonn summit of 1978—on target current-account balances of payments which are consistent with one another. I don't think there has ever been any sort of agreement beyond the idea that it would be a good thing to have such an agreement, but if there is a serious international economic conference following, say, the Williamsburg summit meeting, it ought not only to agree that countries should simultaneously introduce stimulative measures but also to agree on how much is required of each country, because countries are obviously in different economic positions. The United States has been in a special position; because of its size, it has been able to lift and to depress the world economically by its own volition, without any international coordination. This is certainly not true of any other country, and the British example proves time and again that when we expand our economy in order to achieve full employment, we run into balance-of-payments difficulties if our rate of expansion is greater than that of other countries.

The latest example—and a very good example too—is France. The Mitterand government came into power with a Keynesian policy aimed at full employment, with a very expansionary budget which soon brought France into tremendous balance-of-payments difficulties. The government thought it could solve the problem in an orthodox way by devaluing the franc, yet in the next year the current-account deficit was twice as large as in the first year. There was a second devaluation, and that has now been followed by a third devaluation. This time, however, France fell in line with the generally prevailing philosophy of the International Monetary Fund that the proper way to deal with mass unemployment is through deflation. This is something that I could never understand, but there we are.

But I don't wish to talk too much. I just wish to say that, apart from the national aspects of coordinated recovery, there is a purely international reform. I think it has been proved conclusively that, in a global setting, governments and central banks do not have complete control over their respective money supplies. I think it has also been proved that limiting the money supply does not guarantee that a country gets rid of inflation, because inflation in recent years has been fed mainly by the extraordinary behavior of commodities, whose prices have soared at the slightest sign of increasing demand.

To deal with this problem, I am in favor of the old Keynes proposal for an international buffer-stock scheme extending to the major commodities. I would link the proposal to the SDR. My currency reform would relate to an international reserve currency, not to national currencies. Under the arrangement, SDRs would be allotted to countries, not, as now, in proportion to their IMF quotas, but as a result of commodity purchases by the IMF—or by an agency of the rank of the IMF—from the various national buffer stocks. Such purchases would prevent a fall in commodity prices, would increase world investment, and would thereby impart an automatic expansionary stimulus. Or, if prices were too high, commodities could be sold in exchange for SDRs. For monetarists, the important thing is that money is withdrawn from circulation, but for nonmonetarists— the Keynesians—the same story can be told by saying that world investment is reduced. That kind of investment operates with a very high multiplier, under which the pressure of demand of the manufacturing sectors of all the industrial countries is reduced. So this proposal could act as a very powerful stabilizer.

My last remark, which is more controversial than those I have already made, is that I differ fundamentally from the mainstream of economics as represented by the neoclassicists or by followers of the Walrasian model. I don't think that the availability of resources, as such, determines something like a full-employment output or that competition between factors leads to a situation in which anybody who wants a job will find a job unless prevented by trade unions from offering a full-employment wage. I don't believe that; I believe that there is imperfect competition—not perfect competition. In this connection, there is an extremely able and shrewd article by Professor Weitzman of MIT which some of you may have read in the December 1982 issue of the *Economic Journal*. It shows that, given the conditions of imperfect competition, the world economy or the economy of any particular country can get stuck at almost any level of stagnation, because there is no force to cause it to expand, even though labor may be cooperative. But it is time for me to stop.

*Otmar Emminger*: Lord Kaldor has laid so many problems on the table that we could talk about them the whole day, or even longer. I shall not touch on all the issues he raised, but may I first say a few words on his very important initial point—that what the world needs, or may need, is a coordinated approach to economic expansion. This, of course, will be one of the major subjects at the Williamsburg summit conference. I will just say a few words about the probable German position on that, because, as Lord Kaldor rightly said, there will immediately be the question of the contributions of the various countries. You are all aware of the familiar formula according to which those countries should expand which have had the most success in fighting inflation and which have a sound balance of payments on current account. Inevitably, three or four countries are mentioned: Japan, Switzerland, Germany, and some smaller countries; I leave out the United States, because that is always a case by itself.

Now the position of Germany in all likelihood will be negative, or at least very reluctant, with respect to this approach. Not that Germany won't go ahead with the others, but it is certain to repudiate a "locomotive" role. And this for two reasons. First, we burned our fingers as a result of the Bonn summit of 1978, when Japan and Germany were condemned to act as locomotives. This turned out to be a wrong move—very wrong from the German point of view and not even very good from an international point of view. It may perhaps interest you that our former Chancellor Schmidt, who—very much against my advice—agreed to go along with this for purely political reasons, later admitted in an interview in an American magazine that it was one of his worst mistakes. So there is this history against that.

By the way, let me remark in passing that I am not aware that the Bonn summit resulted in much of an agreement on targets for balances of payments on current account. And I can tell you that when I was chairman of the OECD balance-of-payments committee for over ten years, we tried again and again to discuss balance-of-payments targets, and it was just a frustrating exercise.

But let me come back to the German position on this international endeavor to get coordinated action for expansion. There is a second reason why our people would be very reluctant to take any leading part in such a program, and that is the present fiscal position of Germany. At the present time, Germany is in a situation of conflict between short-term cyclical and longer-term structural policy requirements. To be more precise, we are emerging from a serious recession which began in the spring of 1982. We are slowly—but only very slowly—recovering, and that would of course mean that some expansionary stimulus from the budgetary side would be appropriate and welcome. But we are also emerging from a series of years in which we have accumulated very large budget deficits and a huge public debt. Thus there is a structural need for cutting down these excessive public deficits, which at the present time are of the order of about 4.5 percent of GNP.

Now how has the German government up to now dealt with this conflict between short-term and longer-term needs? I think that, consciously or unconsciously, the government has simply gone on a compromise path by accepting the cyclical deterioration of the budget while at the same time trying to cut down the structural part of the deficit. The outcome up to now has been that the overall size of the deficit, say in 1983, will be more or less the same as in the previous year. There has been no improvement at all, despite the government's condemnation of the previous government's excessive budget deficits. But the composition is different; there is more of a cyclical part and less of a structural part, because measures have been taken to improve the structural position.

In my view, this is a very good compromise position, but it has already been criticized by those who believe that the structural or long-term needs should have precedence. They want a lower budget deficit, and they have condemned a few expansionary measures, like stimulating house-building, which are admittedly of a purely Keynesian nature. I think that in the present context such stimulative measures are more or less appropriate, although I know that my friend Armin Gutowski, who is sitting near me, has come out very strongly against this Keynesian stimulus.

In any case, you can see what a difficult situation our government is in. But you may ask: What about monetary policy? Would monetary policy be more stimulative, since fiscal policy has lost its freedom of maneuver? Here again, there are strong constraints. Up to a year or half a year ago, it was mainly the high dollar exchange rate that constrained German monetary policy, just as it inhibited British monetary policy and that of other countries. But it may interest you that I don't think the German delegation at the Williamsburg conference will join those Europeans who try to persuade the Americans to lower the dollar exchange rate, because we can live with the present rate; it hurts the American economy much more than ours.

But another constraint on monetary policy has emerged, because, since the beginning of the year, the money-supply figures have grossly exceeded the targets.

*Cooper*: In America?

*Emminger*: In Germany. So in this respect our situation is similar to that facing American Federal Reserve policy, although for very different reasons. One of the main reasons for our excessive monetary expansion has been the speculative crisis with the French franc, which brought about DM 15–17 billion into Germany. This inflow of funds had to be bought up by the Bundesbank [the German central bank], leading to a very large inflation of the money supply. But, again, the Bundesbank has been criticized by those who think they have the right religion in monetary policy—namely, the 100 percent monetarists. They say that the Bundesbank should not have lowered its interest rate in March as much as it did in view of the excessive expansion of the money supply. So this recent development has become an absolute obstacle to any further expansionary move by the central bank. Indeed, the Bundesbank has had to do the opposite; it has had to reduce the liquidity of the banking system in order to get back on its monetary target.

I am not against this policy of trying to absorb the excessive liquidity; it is going to be absorbed anyway, because most of the inflow of foreign exchange during the recent speculative crisis has already moved out. In fact, I have made a bet with some of the critics of the Bundesbank that within a few months the money-supply figures will be back within the target.

But, for the time being, both fiscal policy and monetary policy are prevented from contributing very much to international expansion—at least not in a deliberate coordinated way. At the same time, there are some very positive elements in our economy. We are benefiting from the decline in oil prices, as are all other oil-importing countries. We are also benefiting from a very reasonable round of wage increases this spring, averaging around 3 percent. These and some other factors may lead to a recovery that is somewhat stronger than predicted at the beginning of the year. That may help the rest of Europe and the rest of the world, but there will not be a deliberate expansionary policy.

*Cooper*: Just one point of clarification. When you speak of Germany's monetary targets, am I right in thinking that these are base-money targets? Or are they M-1?

*Emminger*: No, no; we have always been absolutely against any M-1 target. From the very beginning—we began in 1974, so I know what I'm talking about—we have declined to use M-1, because it was too erratic, even before these erratic movements in 1981. Instead, we have used what we call the central bank money stock, which is similar to base money.

*Cooper*: Then one further question on that. I have read some place that the demand for German currency, which is an important component of base money, has grown exceptionally rapidly. Is that a correct report and, if so, what would you say about it?

*Emminger*: No, it is not a correct report, because it assumed that foreign-held D-marks are included in this money-supply target. They are not; only domestically-held D-marks are included.

*Cooper*: If you're talking about currency, how do you know?

*Emminger*: You mean paper money?

*Cooper*: Bank notes, yes.

*Emminger*: Of course you are right about that. As to bank notes, we have only a vague impression, because there is a rough statistical measure of bank notes sent to German banks from abroad. But you are right; this is something which nobody can know for certain. Bank notes played a great role in 1978 when we overshot our monetary target, because at that time several billion D-marks in bank notes went abroad and, later on, came back. So the money supply was incorrectly estimated. But I don't think that bank notes play a great role now.

*Cooper*: At the present time?

*Emminger*: A minor role, but not a very great role. But as concerns the rest of the money supply, we do not count foreign deposits held in German banks.

*Giovanni Magnifico*: After the statements of Lord Kaldor and Dr. Emminger, I realize that I am going to propose something which is outside the mainstream of the discussion, because what I would like to suggest is that we reflect on the causes of what I fear is a most important change in the last few years—the deterioration in long-term expectations. Those who are at least my age around this table will remember that in the 1950s and 1960s hardly anybody in official or academic circles expressed a doubt about the ability of government to control the business cycle or to promote economic growth. It was assumed that growth would be sustained in the long term and it would absorb unemployment. I remember that when I was stationed in the United Kingdom, people there actually thought that a rise beyond 4 percent unemployment was not really conceivable.

Those days are gone, and we are now faced with a crisis of expectations. This is the result of the global economic instability in the 1970s, as exemplified both in the monetary variables and, of course, in the real variables. In the 1950s and 1960s, we were able to reconcile growth and stability—monetary stability, price stability, exchange-rate stability. Later, we had to be content with trading off inflation and unemployment, which meant, of course, that we found ourselves in a situation in which we had both inflation and unemployment. More recently, most industrial countries have succeeded in bringing down the rate of price inflation, but long-term inflationary expectations do not seem to have subsided. This is one reason, as I understand it, why the U.S. monetary authorities have felt that they could not do much more than they have done to let interest rates come down.

Now why have long-term inflationary expectations not subsided? Is it because of a lack of discipline in the system—or, more particularly, a lack of institutions that are perceived as essential to what one might call a sound monetary constitution? Would a reinstatement of gold in the monetary system help expectations of long-term stability and allow a lower and less volatile level of real interest rates? I know that this is a very controversial issue, and there are those who think that more conventional measures might do the trick. Some of these measures have been mentioned this morning—monetary restraint, coordination of expansion at the international level, and so on. Of course, there would be something to gain in many countries, including some of the major ones, by shifting the burden of fighting inflation from monetary policy to fiscal policy, though Dr. Emminger has explained how both monetary and fiscal policy now have constraints that make them of little use in coping with inflation, at least in the German case.

But the point I would like to raise now is whether there are techniques within the monetary field that can reduce the inefficiency of macroeconomic policies. Would it be possible, for example, to improve monetary policy by aiming at a sort of target zone for the real rate of interest? This raises other questions. Are positive real rates of interest a sufficient condition against inflation if we try to constrain them within a target zone? That is to say, would they make a sufficient contribution to fighting inflation by reducing the demand for credit on the part of those potential borrowers who have an elastic demand—and, perhaps equally important, by exposing the inflationary working of budgetary policy, public expenditure being notoriously inelastic with respect to the interest rate?

Finally, what are the implications of high interest rates for the developing countries and for the debt predicament in which they find themselves? Is the bailing out of the LDC debtors being carried out by a lopsided recourse to commercial banks and to international money creation? And, if so, should we not aim at market forms of refinancing and funding the short-term debt—for instance, by having an international institution, such as the World Bank, that would issue bonds for the world capital market, and, on a case-by-case basis, would grant a long-term loan to a country that had addressed itself to the IMF? The country which obtained such a loan would use it to repay its short-term external debt.

I would like to hear the views of others here about whether the policy measures I have hinted at would help to overcome our crisis of expectations.

*Armin Gutowski:* Several issues have already been touched on here that have been widely discussed elsewhere, but not resolved, and they are all interrelated. As for the present situation, there is clear evidence that a recovery is under way in the United States. In Europe, the forward indicators have also turned upward. Inflation has come down faster than expected, and oil prices have fallen in real terms, but exchange rates still are not fully in line with underlying basic factors. Meanwhile, some politicians are quite satisfied that, with recovery, many of our problems will be resolved more easily than had been expected. But one must not be too optimistic. In Germany, for example, even if the recovery were to bring about full employment of our productive capacity, we would still have more than a million—probably a million and a half—unemployed workers instead of the 2.3 million we have right now.

So that is the short-run picture. But we shouldn't lose sight of longer-run problems. Not only among politicians, but also among economists, there has developed a great deal of uncertainty about the effects of specific policies. First of all, there are doubts concerning monetary policy. There are quite a few monetarists—and also Keynesians—who doubt that their policy prescriptions would really succeed in what they are aiming at. There is an increasing feeling that it is not just monetary aggregates that do the trick, nor is it just interest rates; one has to look at both, as many policy makers are now saying. And in looking at monetary aggregates, one must look at what is happening to all the subgroups: base money, M-1, M-2, M-3, and so on. The same goes for the spectrum of interest rates.

There are also doubts, of course, about fiscal policy. We are no longer as confident as we were of the significance of budget deficits—in particular, the deficit of the United States. Perhaps we have learned the lesson that it is not only the aggregate deficit itself but what kind of expenditures are being made and what kinds of taxes are in effect—the *structure* of expenditure and of taxation. Thus, a truly sophisticated supply-side view would be not just to deal with aggregates but to look at, let's say, the effect on investment stimuli of changing the tax structure rather than reducing the level of taxes. As an aside to Otmar Emminger, it is true that I've said that our housing program in Germany, exactly for the reasons I've just given, is not the best policy—not just because it's Keynesian but because it is building up consumption assets. And that means it is not productive; we have to pay for it out of current income, but it won't really increase the stream of income.

But that's only an aside. We also have to look at these policies and the proper policy mix not only from the point of view of our domestic economies but also in relation to the development of other economies. This means that the "best" mix of monetary and fiscal policies for a particular country might not be the best solution if we take into account the interplay of all the relevant economies in the world.

Here there are more doubts. Even those who were very much in favor of leaving exchange rates to market forces now feel that flexible rates overshoot and undershoot for too long a period, thus having an impact on the real economy and therefore calling for central bank intervention—not just to flatten out very short-term fluctuations, not just to "lean against the wind," but to take into account the different risk assessments in the foreign-exchange market that might run counter to fundamental developments. I myself am in favor of such intervention, and this has been proposed in a recent study, in which I was involved, of the Group of Thirty, entitled *The Problem of Exchange Rates: A Policy Statement.*

In addition, we have to deal with the problem of how we should treat shocks which come from outside our countries. In this connection, there are discussions right now on the impact of lower oil prices. Some even fear that the reduction of oil prices is detrimental to overall economic development. I do not share that view; on the contrary, I am convinced that the fall in oil prices is rather helpful right now. But we do need to look at the question of oil prices in the longer run and of how—whether by import levies or consumption taxes or whatever—we can achieve a more stable price trend for the oil user.

Finally, we have the LDC debt problem. We have proposals on the table like the one of Giovanni Magnifico, who is with us, and the one of Peter Kenen. There are other plans that don't go as far. One of the key questions here is the role to be played by the International Monetary Fund. Another question is whether we should have schemes simply for rescheduling these debts or whether we should go further and write some of them off.

This is all I want to say as an introduction. I have merely provided a rather long list of problems without attempting to solve them.

*Robert Triffin*: Well, I'm sure of one thing: You don't want me to rehash for the millionth time my fundamental diagnosis and prescriptions concerning yesterday's Bretton Woods system, anchored on a gold-convertible dollar, and today's crisis-prone monetary system, anchored on an inconvertible paper dollar. Let me simply say that the events of the last twenty four years have not induced me to modify basically the warning and suggestions which I gave to the U.S. Congress in October 1959. Events seem to me to have confirmed the views I expressed at that time, although the so-called Triffin dilemma was rapidly solved in the direction with which we are all too familiar—an inflationary flood, rather than a deflationary shortage, of international monetary reserves. Measured conservatively in SDRs, with gold at SDR 35 an ounce, world reserves have multiplied by well over four times in a brief span of thirteen years—from SDR 79 billion at the end of 1969 to SDR 364 billion at the end of 1982. Foreign-exchange holdings account for 89 percent of this increase, with SDRs and IMF transactions accounting for the rest (gold holdings in physical terms declined slightly). Measured in dollars, with gold valued at market prices, global reserves increased by almost seven times during the same period.

The enthusiasts of floating exchange rates and of gold demonetization tell me, of course, that such figures are totally meaningless, since exchange profits on gold and foreign-exchange holdings have been sterilized by central banks and thus have not caused an inflationary increase in money supplies. This may be true, but if well established historical precedents are followed in the future, these so-called profits will not be sterilized indefinitely by central banks. In one way or another, as always in the past, they will sooner or later be passed on to the national treasuries, enabling governments to finance bigger budget deficits and to continue the inflationary process in an endless vicious circle.

It would be unkind to remind our ministers of finance and central bank governors of what they repeatedly proclaimed in the initial years of their debates on international monetary reform. They were ready, they said, to negotiate any and all desirable reforms of the system except two, which, they said, were not negotiable: stable exchange rates and a stable official gold price at $35 an ounce; these were to remain unshakable pillars of any future international monetary system. Yet floating exchange rates and a floating price for gold were the major reforms actually implemented in the ensuing years. I shall therefore accept only with several bags—rather than grains—of salt the pronouncements of our officials about the future of the international monetary system.

What I want to stress, though, is that when I think that one of the richest countries in the world is expected to have a merchandise trade deficit of over $60 billion this year—Mr. Feldstein puts the figure at $75 billion—I cannot be as optimistic as Dr. Emminger.* If exchange rates are maintained where they are, as Dr. Emminger seems to wish, I can only foresee extremely powerful protectionist pressures in the United States. So I cannot see this issue simply from the point of view that Europeans may not suffer, or even may benefit, from a situation that is untenable for the United States.

*Robert A. Mundell*: I'm glad to have the floor after Robert's fine groundwork. His statement supports what I've long maintained—that the most significant economic fact of the decade of the 1970s is the breakdown in monetary discipline. There was the breakdown in discipline for countries that abandoned pegged exchange rates, and, for the United States—the principal reserve-producing country—there was the breakdown in discipline resulting from the suspension of convertibility of the dollar into gold.

This collapse of discipline has had very undesirable side effects. One of these has been a ratchet effect involving the gold price, the oil price, other commodity prices, and wages. We've seen two big rounds of oil-price increases; these have been accommodated by the Eurobanks, which in turn have been accommodated by the Federal Reserve. The result has been an immense amount of inflationary monetary expansion. And there's no constraint in the system; the constraint has to be in some form of control over international reserves.

The inflation has led to the growth of debt in countries that are never going to be able to repay that debt. The $700 billion in Third World debt that now exists can't be repaid under foreseeable conditions, and in order to maintain even paper solvency at some of the

---

*The actual U.S. merchandise trade deficit in 1983 (with imports on a c.i.f. basis) was $69.3 billion.

creditor banks, the debt is going to have to be accommodated by even more debt. We're not going to get a correction of the debt crisis; we're going to increase the debt, because the only way that countries like Mexico and Brazil and Argentina can remain solvent is by getting them further into debt. And the loans will be forthcoming, because nobody in the short run ever wants a crisis.

Now fortunately, the program of Nixonomics, which introduced this floating exchange-rate and floating gold-price system, has not been entirely bad. First of all, there has been some redistribution of world wealth and income in favor of the Third World, thus relieving the northern countries of the need to continue bailing out the low-income countries with huge amounts of foreign aid. A second good thing about Nixonomics has been that it allowed the United States to get rid of a lot of messy exchange controls that it had earlier on, and it also allowed the United States to get rid of the iniquitous prohibition on the holding of gold by U.S. citizens—an odious thing for a country that was and is the leading world financial center. As a consequence, of course, we've had a much higher price for gold. But with the freeing of the system, the LDCs, as Eddie Bernstein said, were for the first time getting the liquidity they wanted.

Now the good part is that they got the liquidity; the bad part is that they got themselves into debts they can't repay. And the upshot of that is that the debts are going to have to be either inflated away or forgiven. Inflation may be the eventual solution. This would be better than falling into the trap of complete forgiveness of the debts, which would create a moral hazard for all the credit creation in the future.

But inflation, of course, has left us with enormous problems. It has left us with an inflation premium built into interest rates, and has brought us to a position where we don't seem to be able to manage without a high level of unemployment. Inflation no longer reduces unemployment; it seems to exacerbate unemployment. Inflation and unemployment rates, if not at an all-time high, have been far in excess of what they were under the Bretton Woods system. Back in the 1960s, we worried about unemployment rates as low as 5 percent; now we have unemployment rates of 10 or 11 percent, and almost nobody—Keynesians or monetarists—have any policies that can really be expected to get unemployment in the United States back to the 3 or 4 or 5 percent level that is technically possible with a sensible monetary policy.

Now we don't have to lay too much blame on individuals for this mismanagement. I think Armin Gutowski has done us all a good service with what just has to go down in history as his "doubts speech," because it was filled with doubts about the function of fiscal policy, about the meaning of monetary policy, about the people who created these policies, and about *their* doubts regarding those policies. And that's a good thing; it shows that economics is beginning to grow up a bit—to get out of its diapers if not out of its rompers. We have to start thinking again, and that's a happy thing for all of us.

Let me mention one or two subjects that I would like to hear discussed at this meeting. First, I would like to hear the comments of other members about the working of the floating-rate system and about its relation to the breakdown of monetary discipline. Second, I would like to hear more about the Third World debt crisis, which promises to become increasingly serious. In this connection, I would like to hear more about Giovanni Magnifico's plan; I know he has to go to Basel tomorrow, so it would be good to hear something about his plan while he's here. Third, I think we might give some thought to the instability of the price of gold and the effect of that on the dollar value of international monetary reserves. During a three-week period in January, a decline in the gold price caused a $100 billion drop in the dollar value of international reserves, and, last July and August, the value of such reserves went up by $200 billion when the price of gold went from $300 to $500 an ounce. Fourth, there is the problem of getting interest rates down. We're certainly not going to have a lasting thorough recovery at interest rates that are 10 percent or more. Interest rates have just got to be brought back to 5 or 6 percent—I'm talking now about long-term rates—and the only way they can be brought down to that level is through stabilization of exchange rates and stabilization of the price of gold.

Contrary to many of my colleagues, I think that Reaganomics has had one great success, and that has been the tax cuts that were introduced. I'm glad to see that nobody is really arguing that the United States should take back the tax cuts—the 30 percent tax cuts—that the Kemp-Roth bill established. Actually, the reduction was only 23 percent, but it was a good step. I think we need to do this again; it was so good that it should be done again to keep the recovery going. In 1984 we should have another tax cut of 10 percent, and in 1985 still another 10 percent tax cut. That goes against the monetarists in the administration, but they've been wrong for ten years; it's time that the supply-side advocates have a chance to be right for two more years.

Now, on the exchange system, I think our solution is to return to stable exchange rates and a fixed price for gold. We had a system, the Bretton Woods system, that had defects in it, and it got to a point where the price of gold was ridiculously low. But the lid has come off the boiler on that, and the new price of gold should be set at a much higher level. We don't need to discuss here what the actual gold price should be, but I do think we have to move toward a more stable exchange-rate system—something like the Bretton Woods system, under which most countries pegged their currencies to the dollar, whereas the United States, under the old IMF Article IV, 4(b), intervened in the gold market rather than in the exchange market. We need to have a new Bretton Woods conference—well prepared—and I agree with Nicky Kaldor that it should establish a Keynes-Triffin type of world central bank, old-fashioned style, using a stabilized gold price and an international currency. I think that's the wave of the future and that's what our goal should be in the long run.

# Issues in Recovery: Other Views

*Chairman Cooper*: Many hares have been set loose this morning, and now our task is to chase them down. Who would like to comment? Conrad Jamison wants to say something.

*Conrad C. Jamison*: Bob Mundell made some remarks about debt with which I agree 100 percent. If, in the years ahead, any factor is to drag the world down, it may well be the growing burden of international debt—particularly the debts of the less-developed countries. Too large a portion of these debts is not offset by earning assets; too much has been used to buy food or fuel, which is consumed and gone forever. But the debts remain, getting larger and larger, and in some cases virtually impossible to repay. So this is a basic problem in the years ahead and one of the major threats to international stability.

*Cooper*: Could I interrupt there just to report a result which some of you may know of. Jeffrey Sachs, my colleague at Harvard, did a cross-sectional analysis of the debt acquired between 1973 and 1981, and it shows that the overwhelming portion of the debt went into investment—not into consumption. Now that doesn't mean every loan, of course, and it doesn't mean every country, but it does mean that the increase in investment ratios is highly correlated with the amount of debt acquired.

*Jamison*: Well, some of the borrowing has been used for food and fuel—that's gone—and some has gone into investments which aren't very productive: into national airlines or steel mills that aren't very efficient or necessary. So I think in many cases the assets are not real economic earning assets.

*Triffin*: Are armaments also investment?

*Cooper*: No, no; this is investment as defined in the national accounts.

*Kaldor*: May I make a remark on this problem? The excuse for the sudden outburst of international lending was the recycling of the current-account surpluses of the OPEC countries. But what happened was that, whereas a hundred developing countries suffered a sudden increase in their current-account deficits owing to the rise in oil prices, most of the lending activity was concentrated on the so-called creditworthy developing countries, which were very few—less than a dozen. I want to support what Richard Cooper said a moment ago. To say that these were unsound investments would be very wrong; in fact, the rise in exports of these countries shows that they were very sound investments. But of course the terms of the loans—with short periods and with variable interest rates—were such that when American interest rates went up under the new American policies, the countries got into payments difficulties that were not foreseen, because the annual service burden became enormously larger than had been contemplated. But I fully agree that, as international loans, they went mainly for investment purposes and not just for consumption.

*Cooper*: In any case, the loans pose a serious problem now and, as Bob Mundell suggested, some will have to be written down one way or another, either through inflation or more explicitly, because the borrowing countries are close to insolvency; they cannot carry their debts even under improved economic circumstances. I'd like now to call on Sven Arndt.

*Sven W. Arndt*: As always, Bob Mundell made a number of provocative suggestions. During the coffee break, I offered to support him as president of the proposed world central bank, but he declined—not on substantive grounds, but because the hours didn't suit him.

Let me comment on one point that Bob raised. He observed correctly that unemployment rates, on average, now are higher than under the Bretton Woods system, and he seemed to be suggesting that the cause of this higher level of unemployment is the international monetary system itself. While there may be some connection there, I doubt that the blame can be laid so simply on flexible exchange rates. What I think we ought to look at are the structural rigidities, the inflexibilities, in our economies—in particular, the inability of wages, nominal wages, to follow prices down when we go through a period of disinflation, such as we are in now in the United States. If the level of real wages is inappropriate, as I think it is in many countries, that will surely produce employment problems even during a recovery. I think this is a major point, and I'd like to see it pursued further here.

My second point is the issue that Armin Gutowski raised concerning fiscal policy. I agree that there is a lot of questioning going on, certainly in the United States, about the appropriateness of particular monetary and fiscal policy mixes. This often surfaces in connection with the question of whether high interest rates are due to monetary excesses or to other causes. Here it's useful to bear in mind that the exchange markets often give us helpful information in making judgments on whether high interest rates are mainly due to inflationary expectations, inspired by excessive monetary expansion, or to real factors. If it were monetary looseness that was pushing up interest rates, one would expect the country's exchange rate to be declining, whereas if the pressure on interest rates came from the real side, one would expect the currency to be high or rising. This is not an acid test, but it is certainly a helpful bit of information that comes out of the exchange market. In the United States, of course, we have high interest rates and a strong dollar, and I would argue that this supports the view that real credit tightness, real stringencies, rather than expectational factors, are mainly responsible for the high interest rates. There is some evidence, though it isn't yet very solid, that these high interest rates are largely the result of particular budgetary policies. In any case, these matters clearly deserve further consideration.

*Cooper*: Otmar Emminger has a two-handed intervention.

*Emminger*: Just on this question of identifying the main causes of the structural increase in unemployment. I would very much agree that rigidities or inflexibilities in the system had a lot to do with it, but I would add another factor. We have seen in our country—and I think the situation is similar in other countries too—that the rate of investment in the productive sector has gone down in a structural way. In our country now, it's about half of what it was twelve or fifteen years ago as a percentage of gross national product. And one of the reasons, of course, has been the very large structural increase in the share of the national product used by the government; over this period, the share has gone up from 37 percent to over 50 percent, which means that both the social burdens and the tax burdens on the economy have structurally increased. This is a structural factor, not just a cyclical factor.

*Cooper*: Just so we understand the figures, when you talk about the rise in the government share from 37 percent to 50 percent, does that mean government purchases of goods and services?

*Emminger*: Oh, no; it is total government expenditure, including social transfers.

*Cooper*: So it's a gross figure.

*Emminger*: A gross figure.

*Cooper*: It includes some things that could be investment, for example.

*Emminger*: Yes, but the share of government investment expenditure in total expenditure has gone down too.

*Mundell*: It *is* a call on the tax system.

*Cooper*: Yes.

*Arndt*: That's what I want to emphasize. And it really does make a difference what government expenditures are used for. If much of the expenditure went into investment, one would not be nearly as concerned as one would be if it went for other purposes.

*Kaldor*: I would like to ask Dr. Emminger whether any German economist has made a calculation of government expenditure, not in relation to the actual national income, but in relation to what the national income would have been if Germany had continued to grow at the same rate as it did before 1973. I think we would find that there might be some increase in the share of government expenditure, because the productivity in some government sectors, by definition, cannot increase—where output is measured by input—but otherwise the picture might look very different from that painted by Dr. Emminger.

Secondly, a number of American economists, like George Perry at Brookings and Professor Nordhaus at Yale, have made elaborate econometric investigations on investment, and I was assured by them that in every single case they found that the Acceleration Principle explained 99 percent of the behavior of investment. That is to say, investment went down because the *growth* in demand went down. If, in Germany, exports had continued to increase at the same rate as they did earlier, there wouldn't have been this fall in investment. I would be very interested in Dr. Emminger's views on these points.

*Emminger*: My view on your first point: It's of course true that the share of government expenditure in GNP rose in part because the rate of growth of the economy declined. But this was to be expected; it just means that the government sector was unable to adjust to the new period of lower growth. If you go into the details of the increase in government expenditure, you will see that it is nearly all due to increased social expenditure.

*Kaldor*: Yes—to unemployment.

*Emminger*: No, not to unemployment; the increase in government expenditure came before the increase in unemployment. It was due to an extraordinary expansion of social services, which did not take account of the long-term problems of an aging population. And we are bound to have even more problems in the future, because the aging of our active population will bear very heavily on social expenditure. This explains why the present government takes the long-term structural problem so seriously.

*Kaldor*: That I can understand, but so long as Germany has two million unemployed, may I suggest that government expenditure cannot be the cause of the German economy being unable to grow. I would say that your export performance, for example, is far more important, because, in spite of government expenditure, you still have very large reserves of unemployed labor and capacity that could enable you to grow faster than you do grow.

*Emminger*: That is what I call the conflict between the short-term view and the longer-term structural view.

*J. Howard Craven*: My comments are also inspired by Professor Mundell's provocative statement.

First, I would like to say that we can talk about stabilization without assuming that the stabilization of exchange rates and of the payments system requires the return to a more important role for gold. My thinking goes in the opposite direction; the question in my mind is: How can the countries that have large quantities of gold in their reserves work their way out of them?

My second point has to do with interest rates, a matter raised by Sven Arndt. I wouldn't be as ready as he is to play down the role of expectations, at least in the United States. All one needs to do to explain the behavior of interest rates in the United States is to assume expectations of still higher interest rates. And such expectations are far from irrational when one looks at the increasing claim of government on the capital market. U.S. government borrowing has risen from an average of about 15 percent of the total flow in capital markets to three times that much—45 percent—in the fourth quarter of last year [1982]. During the same quarter, corporate flotations were about a third of normal—something less than 5 percent. So the question is whether, when the U.S. economy resumes any kind of substantial growth, a resumption of private-sector demand—on top of the *perceived* government flotations—can take place at present interest rates.

My third point concerns unemployment. The unemployment rate in the United States over a long period has been cushioned by the gradual reduction in working hours. If one goes back to the turn of the century, one will find that the average number of working hours per week was seventy in manufacturing. That figure has been cut in half since then. I'm concerned about the future of the rate at which we can continue to reduce working hours in view of the accelerated pace of innovation, much of which is labor-saving. I believe that the microchips and robots that Professor Meade talks about should be a source of great concern. If we are to avoid heavy technological unem-' ployment, we will have to devise techniques of distributing labor hours in a much more rapid and efficient way than we've seen in the past.

Finally, a word or two on the matter of Third World debt and of the role that might be played by international institutions. I would like to hear a good discussion of the proposal made by Dr. Magnifico this morning. I am thinking particularly of the plight of small banks that were drawn into this lending and that are now in great distress. These banks—many of them—want out, and find it difficult to get out of the consortia in which they have become involved. I believe that if we had something along the lines that were suggested, with an international institution borrowing from the private market and, as an intermediary, making long-term loans to Third World countries under appropriate safeguards, we could avoid a crisis that might really bring the house down.

*Cooper*: Bob has a two-handed intervention.

*Mundell*: I found all of Howard Craven's comments very thoughtful and perceptive. Let me just comment on the relation between budget deficits and interest rates. Now, historically, budget deficits have moved in the opposite direction from interest rates, because, over the cycle, interest rates have been low when deficits have been big—that is, during a depression. At least that was the experience under the Bretton Woods, gold-standard, fixed exchange-rate type of system. I agree with much of Howard's reasoning with regard to future interest rates, but the only way we can remove inflationary expectations and the belief that future budget deficits will just have to be largely monetized is to impose an appropriate monetary rule.

Now under monetarism of the Friedman type or the Beryl Sprinkel type or any other type, the monetary rule is to stabilize the growth of some monetary aggregate. But that hasn't worked. There might be some mystical aggregate that would do the trick, but in practice what has happened is that the monetary aggregate has been changed from time to time: first M-1, then M-1A or M-1B adjusted, then M-2, and M-zero—base money. The stabilization of base money, as I was arguing with Allen Meltzer last week, would work for about ten minutes.

What we need is a believable regime of what monetary policy is going to be—not just this year, not just as long as Paul Volcker is around, not just during the next five years, but over the long run. And the only way we've been able to do that in the past has been through an international monetary system which is controlled ultimately by international monetary reserves. The way to do this with existing international reserves—predominantly gold and dollars—is to stabilize or put a band around the gold. So I agree with Howard's analysis, but he's got to carry it two or three steps down the road, and then he will come out where I come out.

*Giorgio Basevi*: Several of this group, starting with Giovanni Magnifico, have stressed the importance of the Third World debt problem, because it acts as a brake on the recovery of the world economy. I agree that this is a serious problem, and I share the view that cancellation of at least a part of the debt would be a good way to solve it. But I think there is another debt problem which is less evident and less discussed, and that concerns the government debt of some of the developed countries. In such countries as the United States, the United Kingdom, France, Italy, Denmark, and Belgium, government debt—especially the burden of servicing it—is felt by governments as an obstacle to expansionary policy. This may be one reason for the paradoxical situation cited by Lord Kaldor of resorting to deflationary policy in a deflationary situation.

There are two aspects here. One is that in some cases—for example, the United Kingdom—the burden is really due to inflation. If you correct for inflation, the government budget in the British case is not as bad as it looks and, in fact, is possibly in surplus. And yet the government feels that it is in deficit. It is, on paper, and therefore it does not follow a more expansionary policy. A second aspect, which I think applies to Italy and perhaps also to Belgium and Denmark, is where, even after correction for inflation, the government still is in a bad financial situation. Here you can envisage special funding or even cancellation of part of the public debt, because, from a multigeneration perspective, you really don't lose anything if you think of bequeathing wealth to your children in the future. This is a question of the distribution of debt between generations. For some countries— and again I think of my own country, Italy—a policy of dealing with government debt by having an extraordinary refinancing through taxation, or even by cancellation, would do away with a backlog of problems inherited from external shocks. Thus we could start again from scratch on the road to expansion.

*W. M. Corden*: First, I'd like to say something on the present world economic situation, then something on the LDC debt problem, and finally something on the question of international coordination.

On the present situation, it seems to me that we are in a world recession which is government-made, or manufactured by central banks; it's a result of contractionary monetary policies in the three major economies and also in Britain. It has had a bigger effect than I think many people had expected; the adverse effects have been more prolonged. But it has produced one desirable result; it has brought inflation down. In other words, the four countries I'm thinking of—the United States, Japan, Germany, and Britain—have quite deliberately moved along the Phillips Curve, with all the normal consequences, good and bad.

Now I suggest that the advisers to governments didn't always tell the governments clearly how big the move was. People have been surprised both by the rapid fall in inflation and by the rise in unemployment, so we've moved a rather long way along the curve—longer than was intended. But that's what happened. Of course if we believe, as I do, that in the short run Keynesian policies have their Keynesian effects—that the Phillips Curve is nonvertical in the short run— then, with some monetary stimulus, we can move along the curve the other way. And what's likely to happen is that, with some expansion now, employment and output will go up—this is what we all want—and we'll have a short period before inflation goes up, maybe even a few years. Then we'll all congratulate ourselves that we've reached this marvelous era of low inflation and high employment.

But the big question mark is a year or two hence: Will inflation go up again? The answer hinges crucially on inflationary expectations. Here there seem to be two separate factors. On the one hand is the memory of previous inflations. On the other hand, there is the possible determination by the key governments that they don't want another inflation. If wages start to rise, people may feel that governments will pull in the reins again, and if they really believe that, then we may not get the wage increases. What we economists can contribute is that if wages do start rising again rapidly, once we get a recovery, then we will all support the government pulling in the reins once more.

Going more deeply, it seems to me that our central economic problem today is the high rate of unemployment; if we talk about world recovery, we're talking, above all, about reducing unemployment. Here the chief source of concern is the structural unemployment that is due to real-wage rigidity in relation to productivity changes. That seems to me the most distressing form of unemployment in European countries, in Canada, and in Australia, though not so important, I think, in the United States or in Japan. This type of

unemployment in my own country of Australia, where I spend my
time preaching about it, I call "union voluntary unemployment"; it's
involuntary on the part of the poor people who are unemployed, but
it's created by the trade unions insisting on certain levels of real
wage.

How we solve that problem, I don't know. Let me give you some
figures, taking Australia as an example; I believe exactly the same
figures apply to Germany. Until 1973, we had 1½ to 2 percent unemployment. Then, after 1975, we settled at 4½ to 6½ percent; that is
the unemployment which resulted from the trade unions insisting on
certain levels of real wage. It's what you might call Friedman's natural rate, except, of course, that there's nothing natural about it; it's
created by unnatural monopolies—the trade unions. At present, we
have 10 percent unemployment in Australia, and the difference between 6½ percent and 10 percent is the bit that we can get down by
Keynesian policies. So there is something that can be achieved there.
But this structural real-wage unemployment seems to me a central
problem for which I don't see a simple solution. People talk about
incomes policies, of course, but how do you actually persuade the
unions to accept the necessary policies?

Could I just continue, Nicky, before you come in, or do you want
to come in on this point?

*Kaldor*: On this point.

*Cooper*: First we have Schröder, then Nicky on just this point.
Then the floor goes back to Max [Corden].

*Schröder*: I agree with Max on wage-induced unemployment, but
I would ask: Isn't it the wage *structure* which is wrong? In particular,
aren't the wages of unskilled labor too high? I think that's an important point.

*Corden*: I agree.

*Kaldor*: Max, are you arguing that real wages are rigid upwards or
only downwards?

*Corden*: Rigid downwards; we want them to go down.

*Kaldor*: But why should they go down if productivity goes up? If
efficiency wages go up, real wages should go up too.

*Corden*: In relation to productivity, real wages are too high. If I
can just talk about the case I know, Australia, my judgment is that
real wages, particularly of the unskilled—and that's Schröder's
point—are too high. It's not a question of whether they've gone up or
down; they are just too high in relation to the marginal productivity
of the relevant people.

*Kaldor*: Which means that marginal productivity has gone down.

*Corden*: Well, it has varied. In some cases, it has gone down; in other cases, real wages have gone up while marginal productivity has stayed constant. The situation has varied with circumstances, but, basically, the labor unions adjust their nominal wages so as to get that level of real wages which leaves them with an unemployment rate that they regard as tolerable. In Australia, this is 5 to 6 percent. Now 10 percent they don't regard as tolerable, so now we have a willingness by unions to accept wage constraints, to accept a decline in real wages. I think what I'm saying also applies to all the European countries, including France.

Now may I come to my next point?

*Cooper*: Well, just on Nicky's point, there is one respect in which marginal productivity went down in the period that Max is talking about. That is, oil prices went up, and this called for a reduction in real wages. Such a reduction actually took place in the United States, but did not take place in Europe. I don't know about Australia.

*Corden*: The curious thing there, if I may comment on that, is that there are two countries, Australia and Canada, which didn't suffer from the oil-price rise. Australia is a net importer of oil but a net exporter of energy because of its coal exports. Basically, we benefited; we didn't suffer a significant fall in real income because of the oil-price rise.

*Cooper*: But labor as a factor of production suffered an adverse movement in its terms of trade. That doesn't mean that the country has to. But unless you have a system that can redistribute to labor, there is an adverse movement in real wages, basically.

*Corden*: In Australia, however, I don't think there is any evidence that the marginal product of labor fell as a result of all the shocks we're talking about. But there is clear evidence that real wages rose. And this brings me back to the point that unions will so adjust real wages that they get the level of unemployment they regard as tolerable. In Australia, that meant a rise in real wages; in Europe, it meant maybe constant real wages. But this is just a hypothesis; one can't really prove it.

*Roland Vaubel*: Let me just point out the possibility that labor productivity may rise simply because real wages are too high.

*Cooper*: That's right.

*Vaubel*: And induce still greater unemployment.

*Corden*: Yes. Now Nicky won't agree with this, but just allow me to assume a downward-sloping marginal-product-of-labor curve, which indicates that if you lower the real wage rate, you raise the level of employment. But it also indicates that if you move up the curve, you get a rise in the marginal product of labor. Thus we have the example of Mrs. Thatcher and others priding themselves on the improved productivity of their country because half of the marginal firms have gone out of business! That's no achievement; it's just a movement up the curve. What we want is a shift in the curve, don't we?

*Kaldor*: You don't believe in Okun's Law?*

*Corden*: Well, I don't believe in any laws, to be quite honest. But let me come now to my next point, which is on the debtor developing countries. It does seem to me that it would be highly desirable to arrange for some long-term loans to the twelve or fifteen countries that we're concerned about at the moment, because it is ridiculous that money should have been lent to them on this very short-term basis when the funds are used for investment—even though not all the investment has been entirely economic or fruitful. Now the World Bank already borrows on world markets, and makes structural loans. One obvious possibility would be for the World Bank to borrow on a much larger scale and then make the needed long-term structural loans.

But there are problems. One of them is the interest-rate question. Ideally, what we should do, I feel, is to make loans at a fixed or predictable real rate of interest—obviously not the nominal rate—because a lot of the present trouble has been caused by the real rate rising quite unpredictably. It's all very well blaming the Brazilians and the Mexicans, but the fact is that, five years ago, none of us predicted these high real rates. But another problem is that if the World Bank or some other institution takes on this role, there is a risk element; countries can default. Presumably, this means that ultimately the taxpayers of the major countries will have to back these loans. Now these are the realities; I'm still in favor of the loans, but one has to think these things through.

Now I come to my last point, and I'm not going to take much longer. What I'm puzzled about is the talk about international coordination of policies for economic expansion. Now is it not possible for a country such as France, if it believes in Keynesian policies, to print more money and have a demand expansion that would result in a depreciation of the franc and higher employment—but at the cost of

*Okun's Law refers to the relationship between the growth rate of real gross national product and the level of unemployment; e.g., if the growth rate of real GNP is increased by $X$ percent, unemployment will fall by $Y$ percent.

the higher inflation that we all know goes with moving along the
Phillips Curve? The French are free to do this. If they did it, but soon
stopped, would it not be because they didn't like the inflation?

*Kaldor*: I'm sure you're wrong in the French case.

*Corden*: Well, that may not be the best example, but I can't help
feeling that the recession we've been living through has not been
caused primarily by transmission from a weakened United States to a
wonderful Japan and Germany; it has been caused by independent
policies in each country which are the result of intellectual transmission. What I mean is that all the main countries, with a few exceptions, have *chosen* to be somewhat monetarist and deflationary in
their policies, because they are all reacting to the same problems in
the same way. Possibly OECD meetings and the like lead to this intellectual transmission, but a country can do its own thing, if it
wants to, and everybody is afraid of inflation.

*Cooper*: Yes, but isn't it possible that independent national action leads to steeper Phillips Curves than would collective action? To
put the matter another way, isn't it likely that individual choices
don't add up to the same choice that would be made if people faced a
collective, less steeply sloped Phillips Curve?

*Corden*: Implicit in that view is that if one country expands by
itself, it tends to worsen its terms of trade.

*Cooper*: That's right.

*Corden*: Yes, but that raises another question. Suppose the
United States expands through monetary expansion. This would tend
to improve the terms of trade of other countries and thus make it
easier for them to expand. I think there's something in that. Obviously, if the United States were to expand and thereby to improve the
terms of trade of the developing countries and of Australia and
Canada—the primary-product exporting countries—then commodity
prices would tend to rise in relation to the prices of manufactured
goods. It's not obvious that a U.S. expansion would improve the
terms of trade of Germany and Japan, because it would tend to raise
the price of oil, the price of copper, food prices, and so on, and that
would have an effect in the other direction. So whether it's really in
the interest of the industrial countries to urge one another to expand
is questionable because of these commodity-price effects.

*Cooper*: I have a reply to that, but now is not the time for it. Let
me just say that I think you focused on the wrong aspect in raising
the subject of commodity prices. Bob Heller is next on my list.

*H. Robert Heller*: A great deal has been said here about the LDC
debt problem, but it is important to get the figures straight. One sees

figures as high as $600 billion, but the net amount owed to banks is only about $50 billion for the developing countries as a whole. If we look at the non-oil-exporting countries as a separate group, the figure is about $150 billion. So the net burden of servicing the debt is much smaller than the $600 billion figure would imply.

*Mundell*: How do you get such a low figure?

*Heller*: For the banks?

*Mundell*: How do you get from $700 billion down to $50 billion?

*Heller*: You mean $600 billion.

*Mundell*: That figure is out of date; it's $700 billion now.

*Cooper*: Grant Heller his $600 billion, and the question still stands: How does he get from $600 billion down to $50 billion?

*Heller*: The $600 billion is the total debt of the developing countries to international institutions, commercial banks, suppliers, and other creditors. If we look just at the LDC debt to commercial banks, we get a figure of about $300 billion. Now, for commercial banks, we have data on LDC assets and liabilities; the assets amount to about $250 billion, and the liabilities, as I have just indicated, amount to about $300 billion. So the net borrowing by the developing countries from the commercial banking system amounts to about $50 billion— $47 billion as of the end of 1981.

*Cooper*: But you're including OPEC in the developing countries.

*Heller*: That's right. If you take OPEC out and look only at the non-oil-developing countries, the figure is about $150 billion, which is the net amount that has to be serviced. This is really a better indicator of the magnitude of the problem. And don't forget that a lot of the debt, such as that held by the World Bank, is at concessionary interest rates—6, 7, 8 percent. That's not the debt which is responsible for the problem we have now.

*Kaldor*: But the figure I've seen for the accumulated financial surplus of the OPEC countries is $300 billion, not $150 billion.

*Cooper*: But that's not all in the banking system; Bob is dealing just with figures in the banking system.

*Heller*: My data are from the Bank for International Settlements. Now Bob Mundell has told us that the one thing we should do about the debt is to inflate it away.

*Mundell*: I didn't say you *should* inflate it away; I said that ultimately it *will* be inflated away.

*Heller*: You said either inflated away or forgiven, right? Those were your two options. But inflation doesn't eliminate the problem when the debt is at floating rates of interest. Instead, inflation even increases the debt-service problem, because suddenly the debtor

countries have to make greatly increased interest payments before
the loans mature.

But the debt problem should be looked at in perspective. If you
correlate the growth of the international assets of commercial banks
with the growth of world trade, you will find that the two trends are
almost congruent; one is right on top of the other. For the world as a
whole, you get a correlation coefficient of .98—the sort of figure you
usually get only in communist elections. So the growth in international debt has not been out of line with the growth of international
trade.

*Kaldor*: May I ask a question? Is it not true that in 1973 the
American banks had a reserve-to-liability ratio of 9 percent and now
they have one of 3 percent?

*Heller*: No; since the early 1970s, the ratio has barely moved.
The statistics on that have been published by the International Monetary Fund in one of its Occasional Paper series. You will find that
the ratio deteriorated very slightly during the 1970s, but that since
1979 it has improved ever so slightly. You do find very significant
differences internationally if you look, say, at the French banks, the
Japanese banks, or the German banks.

*Mundell*: If what you say is true of American banks, why are
banks like yours—the big commercial banks—collecting such exor-
bitant rescheduling fees? It seems to me that you have very much of
a vested interest here. I know that there's a great deal of competition
among the top three American banks over who gets these fees, which
are just enormous and which add substantially to the debt burdens of
the developing countries. I'm really surprised to hear you say that the
LDC debt crisis is not much of a problem

*Cooper*: Bob, would you keep in mind that we have not let Heller finish, so we don't know where he's coming out.

*Heller*: I'm torn between finishing and going right after Bob now.
Let me finish first. So much of the new indebtedness, as Dick Cooper
has pointed out, has gone into new investment in the developing
countries, and that has created much of the difficulty that we have in
the industrialized world today. When American steel workers or
American automobile workers are bargaining for higher wages, they
are really bargaining themselves out of a job vis-à-vis the Japanese or
vis-à-vis the Brazilians.

And there are two different types of unemployment. One involves workers in the high-skilled, high-wage industries, such as au-
tomobiles and steel. The other involves low-skilled workers in the
industrialized countries, who, even with a minimum wage in the

neighborhood of $3 an hour, just cannot compete with unskilled workers in the developing countries. Now there is one way out for the industrialized world—not fewer work hours, because one cannot be competitive internationally by working less—but more investment, leading to greater productivity. Then you don't need protectionism. That's the end of my sermon.

*Hans-Eckart Scharrer*: Let me go back to your remarks on LDC debt. I'm a bit doubtful whether one really should work with aggregate figures, because the debt problem is confined to a rather small number of developing countries. You risk defining the problem away if you use aggregate figures. Moreover, those countries which have not been able to get help from the banks—the least developed countries—are in the paradoxical position of being net creditors of the banks. So in aggregating and netting out these figures, you really make the problem look less serious than it actually may be. I'm in agreement with "dedramatizing" the problem, perhaps, but one should be careful.

*Cooper*: But isn't the other side of what you're saying—with which I agree—that although this is often presented as a global problem, it's really a problem of half a dozen countries.

*Scharrer*: Exactly.

*Cooper*: It's not global in the sense in which we normally use that term, but the half dozen countries are big countries, so that this could become a global problem if something happened to them.

*Heller*: Well, the total GNP of all the countries that have thus far rescheduled their debts amounts to something like 5 percent of world GNP—that's all.

*Cooper*: Max Corden has a two-handed intervention.

*Corden*: I would just like to comment on one possible implication of Bob Heller's argument that I think he happened to miss. The implication is that if a country were to cut itself off from world trade through protection, it could sustain a higher level of real wages. Now that may be true for the steel workers, but, in general, if countries impoverish themselves by losing the benefit of international trade, they will end up with lower real wages—that are compatible with full employment—than in an open world economy. So we should not think that reducing the impact of world trade makes it possible to have a higher level of employment at higher real wages. I'm sure that Bob didn't mean that implication.

*Heller*: No, no, no—not at all; I fully agree with you. Clearly, it is possible to do things so inefficiently at home that you will actually have full employment, because you need the entire working population to do in a very inefficient manner what could be done much more efficiently with fewer workers. But that's no way to attack the unemployment problem.

*Corden*: What about higher real wages?

*Heller*: You won't have higher real wages.

*Cooper*: Bob, can you comment briefly on the question that Mundell raised: Why is it that the big banks charge such heavy up-front rescheduling fees? I think Mundell linked this matter with bank capitalization ratios, and before you answer the question let me try to reconcile Lord Kaldor's observations with yours. You are completely correct for U.S. banking. It is true that for certain banks the capital ratio has declined sharply, but not for all banks. That's my impression from the figures.

*Heller*: Yes, but I don't think you should use the word *sharply*, though there must be some banks for which the ratio has declined.

*Cooper*: The numbers that stick in my mind are not from 9 percent to 3 percent, as indicated by Lord Kaldor, but from 6 percent to 4 percent—the ratio of loans to capital and reserves, including accumulated surplus.

*Heller*: Yes. Let me continue on the subject of capitalization. As you know, there is a big move afoot in Congress right now to force banks to have higher capitalization ratios. One thing generally overlooked—certainly by Congress—is that these higher capitalization ratios are always based on the assumption of other things being equal; other things being equal, the banks will be safer with higher capitalization ratios. But this neglects the fact that banks operate in the capital market, where they have to raise funds for the shareholders. Now if, let's say, the general rate of return in the economy is 10 percent, then banks have to offer that 10 percent rate of return to their shareholders. If banks are forced by law to have a higher capitalization ratio, the only way they can do that is to concentrate their business where higher—and riskier—spreads are available. Consequently, they will no longer lend to the Belgian government with a ⅜ percent spread, because they just can't earn enough of a return in view of the higher capitalization ratio. The banks will pull out of the safest business first in favor of the higher-spread, higher-risk business. And there's no way around that.

Now about the rescheduling fees. A large part of these fees is simply payment for all the management time that is involved in arranging the rescheduling—and it takes a lot of time. I think everyone agrees that in the late 1970s the spreads had become too low, resulting in the slight decline in the capitalization ratios that has been noted here. I see the rescheduling fees as helping to restore more normal spreads after a period in which these had been abnormally low. All you have to do is look at what has happened to bank stocks over the last five years. Until the middle of last year, the value of bank stocks in most cases had dropped by 50 percent, and now that the spreads are rising a little again, bank stocks are beginning to recover. So, yes, the spreads are bigger, the overall level of interest rates is clearly down, and conditions have shifted a little in favor of the banks.

*Gutowski*: Just one point. I didn't find convincing what you said about lending to the higher-risk borrowers, because I am not at all sure that the realized rate of return on such loans is actually higher.

*Heller*: But if somebody tells you that you have to maintain a minimum ratio of 10 percent capital to every dollar of loans out-standing, which loans do you drop first? You drop the loans that don't meet that 10 percent rate of return per dollar of equity.

*Gutowski*: That implies that the realized rate of return on risky investments is, on the average, higher than on nonrisky investments.

*Mundell*: Assuming that Bob Heller's presentation of the debt problem is correct, why have the big banks closed out essential new lending—apart from lending to refinance the loans to Latin America? According to his figures, the banks shouldn't be worried at all; they should just go on doing what they've been doing.

*Heller*: Well, the debt problem was caused by three different factors that impinged on the various countries around the world in different ways. First of all, we had the drastic run-up in real interest rates—and "real" is the key word here. Whereas during the 1970s real interest rates were very close to zero, they had climbed to around 9 percent in 1980, and are still high. So there has been a very sharp increase in the debt-servicing costs of the developing countries, and that clearly hits the largest borrowers the hardest. That's why the largest borrowers went down first—not the little ones. The other two factors have been the stagnation in the volume of international trade and a deterioration of about 25 percent during the past two years in the terms of trade of the developing countries. These three factors fully explain, I think, the debt-service difficulties that the developing countries have experienced.

*Mundell*: But I'm talking about the marginal problem. Why is the IMF managing director having such difficulty in getting the commercial banks to go along with more lending? Why aren't they bringing up the money quickly? They're making big profits on it.

*Heller*: Well, first of all, I thought we just agreed that the debt service of the borrowing countries is in difficulties. So the marginal bank always has an incentive to pull out of such operations. The banks that want to pull out are the small and medium-sized banks that have a couple of million dollars outstanding in each of those countries. For these banks, it is no longer a very profitable business. If you look at the bigger banks—and they're the only banks that publish data on how much they earn by country—it's Citibank that's been doing really well. Citibank revealed that, last year, the Brazilian operation alone earned a net profit of $160 billion. That's approximately one-fourth of Citibank's earnings for the entire year. Now why should the big banks pull out of a thing like that?

*Mundell*: Why have they?

*Heller*: They haven't.

*Corden*: I've always thought of banks as prudent organizations managed by people in dark suits, but what puzzles me is the following. The argument seems to be that risky loans, which naturally get a high rate of interest, are better for banks than less risky loans at a lower rate of interest. But I would have thought that when you make a risky loan, say to Brazil at a high rate of interest, you set aside some money into a fund to allow for the risk, so that when the situation turns sour, you don't have to ask the World Bank or some other institution to rescue you; you rescue yourself. If a bank is so imprudent as to make very risky loans and say, "Oh, isn't it wonderful with these high interest rates; it's all current profit, we can distribute the dividends, live high, eat in fancy restaurants, and so on," it makes one wonder. That's not the proper way of managing, is it?

*Heller*: Well, if bankers behaved that way, you're certainly right.

*Gutowski*: Max is saying, in effect, what I said earlier—that the profit on risky loans is not necessarily higher than on safe loans.

*Cooper*: But, for risk-averse institutions, you would expect the average rate of return on risky investments to be higher than on non-risky investments. Isn't that so?

*Corden*: But if the institutions are risk-averse, they would not want to make risky loans.

*Cooper*: Well, there are some countries, of course, that haven't been able to borrow at all from commercial banks.

*Scharrer*: I would like to get away from the subject of LDC debt and turn to a subject which you, Mr. Chairman, raised at the very beginning of this session—namely, the issue of trade. If we are to talk seriously about global economic recovery, I think we have to address the question of trade protectionism, especially in relation to the highly open European economies, Japan, and—perhaps to a lesser degree, but even there—the United States.

In my view, it's not so much the level of protectionism that we actually have, but it's rather the trend which has developed in the years since the second oil-price shock of the late 1970s. Since then, we have witnessed a number of incidents where governments on both sides of the Atlantic have become increasingly involved in adding to their administrative weapons against imports or against so-called unfair trade practices. When we consider the crucial role of investment in world recovery, I think we have to regard this trend with considerable anxiety, because it acts as a strong deterrent to investment. Enterprises are not likely to find investment attractive when they fear that, because of increasing protection abroad, their market may be shrinking and they may be unable to sell the goods that they can produce with new plant and equipment.

Unfortunately, there are no easy recipes. A key problem in this area is that government has become increasingly involved in taking over responsibility, not only for the economy as a whole, but for particular industries—whether by directly subsidizing them or by taking them over or by enacting restrictive trade legislation in order to shield them against competition from abroad. Such shielding has been applied not only to old established industries but, to an increasing degree, to new industries as well. So, in our discussion of measures to promote global recovery, I think we have to address not only the monetary issues but also the trade issues—particularly in their relevance to investment.

*Cooper*: I think that's a good note on which to close this session. Max Corden talked earlier about the inflation-unemployment trade-off on which we move. One of the trade-offs we may discover in moving down the Phillips Curve is the change in the trading structure and the change in the role of government in our economies, because it is precisely in periods of low capacity utilization and high unemployment that there are tremendous political pressures to salvage particular firms and particular industries. So we end up, possibly, with a very different structure of economic decision-making from the one with which we went in. And that is somehow missing from the Phillips Curve analysis.

# Interest Rates, Budget Deficits, and Supply-Side Economics

*Chairman Cooper*: It seems to me that our opening discussion this morning divides naturally into two—or one might say two and a half—topics.

The first is what one does about the immediate situation— whether it is appropriate to think of "locomotives" or not, whether doing nothing is the best course of action, whether doing nothing is too dangerous and there are some positive courses of action that might be taken. An aspect of that, but not important enough to be identified as a separate subject, I think, is the question of external debt of developing countries and whether that is a sufficiently serious obstacle or drag or threat to recovery that it needs to be addressed as a thing in itself. In any case, there are proposals for dealing with the debt problem which I think might be useful to discuss here.

Then there are the longer-range issues addressed by a number of our opening speakers on the nature of the system—or nonsystem, as Max Corden and others have called it—and whether we have reached the stage, after ten years of floating, when we should think consciously about a new or somewhat reformed international monetary system. If you are agreeable, I would propose that we divide the discussion into those two or two and a half subjects, that we begin this afternoon with the recovery aspects—the more short-term questions—and that we reserve a substantial part of tomorrow for the longer-term issues.

*Triffin*: May I suggest that we would all like to have your views before we adjourn.

*Cooper*: Well, the chairman is supposed to be neutral in these discussions, and I don't want to allow my own views to interfere with the dialogue, but at one point or another I hope to come in with some opinions on these questions.

*Randall Hinshaw*: I'd like to remind the chairman that he is also the moderator—the role traditionally played by Lord Robbins—and that the conference will be the loser if he doesn't give us the benefit of his views whenever he wishes to express them.

*Cooper*: Well, let's get back to business. Armin Gutowski has the floor.

*Gutowski*: I would like to return to the subject of real wages. From the employer's point of view, it is not simply real wages, but rather total real labor costs, which count. In many countries, and particularly in Germany, the nonwage labor costs—including, but not confined to, social-security payments by employers—are very substantial, sometimes running as high as 80 percent of the total cost of labor.

On a related point, I like Max Corden's expression, "union voluntary unemployment." There is also a sort of voluntary unemployment imposed by laws, which are, of course, to a certain extent the result of pressure from unions, but not only from unions. For example, in Germany people can become pensioners at the age of 60 if they can't find employment in the positions they were trained for. They are free, in other words, to be unemployed. In fact, they have the right not to take on jobs if the jobs that are offered are ten or fifteen miles away from where they are living. So there is quite a bit of unemployment which adds to the "natural" unemployment rate because of these developments in my country and in other countries too.

Let me now turn to the relation between real wages and real interest. Real interest rates are so high because we have these huge budget deficits—in particular, the U.S. deficit—and because much of the money borrowed by governments is used, not for investment, but for consumption. Even where the money is used for investment, it is often unsoundly invested. But what should one mean in this connection by "sound" investment? Sound government investment, in my judgment, would mean that the marginal rate of return on capital is at least as high as the return on capital in private investment. And I have the feeling that in many countries this is just not true; in general, we have a very low return on investment in the public sector.

My next point is that we can really live with a high real rate of interest. But we should look at this matter of investment and saving from the point of view of how we treat consumer credit. In the private sector, we deduct consumer borrowing from saving; we say that it is dissaving. The same should hold true for government; if governments borrow for consumption purposes, then we should deduct that from saving.

*Cooper*: It's dissaving.

*Gutowski*: Yes, it's dissaving, and that reduces the supply of capital for productive purposes.

*Cooper*: Exactly.

*Gutowski*: Now back to the question of real wages and real interest. If real interest rates are high, that is another burden on labor, because we have to use a total-cost approach, as Joan Robinson stressed in some of her publications. If the real interest rate is high, that doesn't mean that we have to have unemployment, but it does mean that real wages will have to be lower than they would otherwise be.

What can be done about this? One approach, of course, would be to try in one way or another to reduce nonwage labor costs. At the same time, it is very important that capital should flow to investment with the highest marginal return, and under present conditions I feel that this is mainly private investment, not only in Germany but in many other countries too. But what do we do about workers whose marginal product is low? There is no easy way to get unions not to price such labor out of the market, so we have to think about that problem. One of the ways, I feel, is to change the tax structure. If we had a tax structure with perhaps a negative part to it, that could offer a greater spread for wages, because, for the low-quality worker, the loss in wages would be partly offset by a negative income tax.

*Cooper*: I wonder if I might step out of the chairman's shoes for a moment to say a few words on interest rates—not to make a judgment but just a factual observation. My own view is that it's especially important at a time like this to drop the convention, which is so convenient to theorists and teachers, of talking about *the* interest rate. Instead, we should differentiate between at least three interest rates. One is the short-term rate on relatively riskless assets; in the U.S. context, I have in mind the Treasury-bill rate. A second is the long-term rate on relatively riskless assets—say, twenty-year or thirty-year government bonds. A third is the commercial long-term interest rate.

One of the striking things about the present situation is that the relationship among these three interest rates has changed. In the 1975 recession, the Treasury-bill rate was actually negative in real terms and about 4 percent in nominal terms—half the long-term nominal rate on U.S. government bonds, which was about 8 percent. As was traditional, the rate on high-quality bonds was a half to a full percentage point higher than the government-bond rate.

Today, the real short-term interest rate is exceedingly high. We have no way of observing the real long-term interest rate; it's a guess. But we can observe the real short-term rate, and it is very high; the nominal short-term rate is about 8 percent, and the government-bond rate is about 11 percent. In previous recessions, short-term rates were half or less of bond rates, but this time they are much higher than half of what bond rates are. And the spread between the government-bond rate and corporate bond rates has increased by a factor of about three, which suggests that there is a big risk premium. That spread was especially big in 1982; it is coming down now, but it suggests great risk. And risk here means default risk, basically.

Let me talk about the fiscal year that ended last October [1982]. The United States had a budget deficit that, in its relation to GNP, was no higher than in 1975 or in earlier recessions, yet real interest rates were very much higher. I think it is bad economic history to impute these high real short-term interest rates simply to the size of the government deficit. It's a combination of monetary policy and the budget deficit that's responsible, and I infer that monetary policy has been a lot tighter in this recession than it was in the other postwar recessions.

The long-term interest rate we can argue about indefinitely. The potential determinants are many, but I would suggest that one of the most important determinants of the long-term rate has been the short-term rate. And as long as the real short-term rate is as high as it is, long-term interest rates are not going to come down.

*J. E. Meade*: Would you repeat the figures for present nominal interest rates?

*Cooper*: For U.S. Treasury bills, 8 percent; for long-term U.S. government bonds, 11 percent; for corporate bonds—depending on quality—around 13 percent.

*Mundell*: While I agree with your facts, I'd like to add to the analysis. In differentiating various types of interest rates, we need to make another distinction; we need to distinguish between net-of-tax interest rates and gross interest rates.

*Cooper*: I agree.

*Mundell*: Ordinarily, that relationship may be a constant if the tax structure is constant, but the tax structure on interest rates has changed substantially. The only long-term interest rate that is net of tax in the United States is that on municipal securities. The relation between that rate and other long-term rates has changed. We now have a change in the U.S. tax structure, with a decline in the maximum marginal income-tax rate from 70 percent to 50 percent. Even so, in this tax bracket, the net-of-tax interest rate is only half of the gross interest rate. In any case, there is a muddying in making comparisons—a muddying of short-term and long-term relationships and a muddying of inflation-premium relationships. And real interest rates are really far lower than they appear to be because of the distinction between net-of-tax and gross interest rates.

*Gutowski*: Lower but still high, aren't they?

*Mundell*: Well, if you take 12 percent as the long-term interest rate at the present time, and if interest is taxed at 50 percent, your net-of-tax nominal interest rate will be 6 percent. If, at the same time, you have an expected inflation rate of 6 percent in the long term, the net real interest rate is zero.

*Meade*: Surely in this case what Mundell says is quite right. But the most important effect of taxation is to make a distinction between the real interest rate that the borrower pays and the rate that the lender gains. If you're thinking of interest rates from the point of view of their attraction to savers, then it's the post-tax rate that you want to keep in mind. If you're thinking about interest rates from the point of view of the incentive to invest, then it's the pre-tax rate.

*Cooper*: It's the pre-tax rate unless interest payments are tax-deductible. That's why it gets complex.

*Mundell*: There's an important fact in this connection that explains the large U.S. balance-of-payments deficit on current account. Foreigners, by and large, don't pay a high tax rate on bond income, which means that, for them, the net-of-tax interest rate may be little, if any, lower than the gross interest rate on bonds. The 12 percent gross interest rate in the United States, which may be a net rate for foreigners, is higher than for almost any investments of the same degree of risk in other countries. The result is a large net inflow of capital into the United States, despite the fact that the United States is a capital-rich country. Under the floating exchange-rate regime, the net capital inflow is automatically matched by a corresponding payments deficit on current account. This artificial current-account deficit is likely to continue for a long time to come, because the gross U.S. interest rate is a net rate to foreigners, and that is a terrific rate of return in a currency in which inflation has been stopped, or sharply reduced.

*Cooper*: It's a net rate to foreigners only if they don't have to pay taxes on it. And that suggests that maybe there should be closer cooperation among tax authorities. I have a two-handed intervention by Mr. Matthes; then Dr. Emminger.

*Matthes*: Mr. Chairman, I am somewhat puzzled by your statement that one of the most important determinants of the long-term interest rate is the short-term interest rate. This doesn't correspond at all with our German experience. For example, on March 17 [1983], the Bundesbank lowered the discount rate by 1 percent, and the response was that long-term interest rates, instead of going down, went up slightly. From the Bundesbank's perspective, the step was clearly counterproductive. It revealed a great dilemma—the dilemma of an open economy which is under external constraint and in which inflationary expectations are still vivid. What apparently happened in Germany was that we moved too soon in inducing this short-term interest-rate reduction, with the result that inflationary expectations were revived. That led to an immediate response in the capital market; capital exports in March reached a record level of DM 4 billion on portfolio account—that is, on long-term account—thus causing a new rise in long-term interest rates.

*Emminger*: I'm not sure whether I understood Bob Mundell rightly when he said that there is a capital inflow into the United States in spite of the fact that the United States is a capital-rich country. Bob, did you say that?

*Mundell*: Yes.

*Emminger*: I have always been under a completely different impression. If you look at the net savings rate in the United States—not just household savings but total net savings—and compare that with the part that is absorbed by the federal budget deficit, you will find that in 1982 the federal deficit took away more than 70 percent of U.S. net savings. The total net savings rate—I take it from the president's *Economic Report* of February of this year—seems to be around 6 or 7 percent of national income. This is a much lower percentage than in a number of other countries—especially Japan but also Germany. And as concerns new capital formation, the ratio in the United States is one of the lowest.

*Mundell*: Whether a country is capital-rich or not is a function of its capital stock, not the yearly flow; it's a function of the accumulated capital stock over time.

*Emminger*: Would you not agree that one overall measure of the need for capital is the balance of payments on current account? Since the middle of 1982, there has been a growing U.S. current-account deficit, which means that there is a growing shortage of capital that has to be made good by the import of capital from abroad. And this deficit is going to increase in 1983, as we all know. Doesn't that indicate a shortage of U.S. capital?

*Mundell*: No, it does not; I wouldn't agree. I would say that an important part of the world that we've created, with floating exchange rates and all that, is that countries around the world have to look for safe abodes for their saving. In the 1960s, as you know, a principal abode for liquidity and savings was U.S. Treasury bills and other liquid assets in the United States. In the 1970s, as countries got the liquidity they wanted, they naturally sought higher yields on their investments, and, with the steep rise in interest rates, U.S. government securities have continued to provide a safe and attractive abode for foreign savings. Under these conditions, there is no way in which the United States by any policy, exchange-rate or otherwise, can alter the fact that it has imposed upon itself a current-account deficit. The capital flow into the United States, pressured by the foreign demand for U.S. government securities and other liquid assets, imposes an excess of current-account spending in the United States and a reduction of current-account spending in the rest of the world. It's simply a matter of the economics of transfer.

*Kaldor*: I presume that Dr. Emminger included business savings.

*Emminger*: I did—all savings.

*Kaldor*: Well now, as regards personal savings, there is—and always has been—a very big difference between America and Western Europe.

*Emminger*: I didn't talk about that difference.

*Kaldor*: But that difference accounts for the main difference between Europe and America. It is a fact that in America wage and salary earners spend about 95 percent of their income and save 5 percent, whereas in Western Europe they spend 85 percent and save 15 percent. In the case of business saving, however, I have found, in calculations I have made, that the proportion of gross profits which is saved is just as high in the United States as it is in Western Europe. The difference between the two areas is really in personal saving habits. And a lot of businessmen would maintain that if American wage and salary earners saved more, that would be very bad for business. After all, the whole purpose of the vast amount spent on advertising is to induce people to spend more of their income and to save less. And that is a very sound reason from the point of view of the profitability of enterprise.

*Mundell*: The fact that the flow of total saving in the United States has been high relative to private investment is related to the budget deficit. The recession itself, as we all know, is caused by an excess of saving over investment, and this excess of saving over investment in the United States has to be offset partially by the budget deficit. There's no alternative; it's a matter of national-income accounting.

*Scharrer*: Professor Mundell appears to imply that there is only a limited need by private enterprise to use these savings (namely, 30 percent of the total—the figure cited by Dr. Emminger), so that the remaining 70 percent has to be absorbed by the budget deficit; the U.S. government has to make up the difference. Now one can look at this, of course, from a different point of view, and ask: What is really the residual? If we consider government as being interest-inelastic, then we could simply say that government absorbs 70 percent of the savings, and what is left over goes to business, with business determining the rate of interest. The rate of interest will be high because of the limited amount of saving available to business. And with the interest rate as high as it is, U.S. business cannot absorb more than this 30 percent; only investment with a high rate of return will be profitable.

*Mundell*: I have a comment on that. At the present time, less than three-fourths of existing U.S. plant capacity is being employed, so that people are reluctant to add to that capacity, especially when it's risky. That is one of the principal reasons why one can fairly say that the United States is in a position to export capital; it has a lot of savings to export. It's a capital-rich country on nearly all grounds.

*Cooper*: But Emminger's point was that, since the middle of last year, the United States has become a capital importer.

*Corden*: I also want to comment on this Emminger-Mundell issue. If we assume a small open economy that faces a given rate of interest in the world, then we can look at these matters in the following way. The current-account position in the balance of payments is the net result of private investment, private savings, and the budget deficit. Now the optimal position on current account will be that which results from optimal investment, optimal savings, and the optimal budget deficit. These would be determined by comparing the expected rate of return on private investment with the real rate of interest and, where possible, by doing the same thing with the public sector. And we may end up with a current-account deficit or surplus, which may vary from year to year.

That's for a small economy. When we come to large economies —the United States, Japan, Germany—they of course can influence the world interest rate and the world capital-market equilibrium. Here I would think the dominant consideration should be: the lower the rate of interest, the better for the world—particularly from the point of view of the developing countries but also from the point of view of generally fostering private investment and growth. On these grounds, the U.S. deficit should be much lower.

*Cooper*: Current-account deficit or budget deficit?

*Corden*: I was thinking of the current account. But, as far as the rest of the world is concerned, it doesn't matter whether it's a private-sector or public-sector deficit; the net result is that the United States is going to be borrowing from the rest of the world.

Now the other side of this, which is often neglected, is that we should be delighted when the Japanese want to have a current-account surplus. And, by the same logic, we should welcome the attempts by the Japanese to reduce their budget deficit, because that should tend, if only marginally, to reduce rates of interest in the world and to make more funds available to Brazil, Mexico, and so on. I think these are the sorts of considerations one should think about in dealing with these questions.

*Mundell*: In a full-employment economy.

*Cooper*: I was going to make the same point. Your last point, it seems to me, is absolutely correct in an environment in which resources are fully employed. In that case, you want a Japanese current-account surplus, which represents real investment in the rest of the world. But in an environment in which capacity utilization rates are around 70 percent in the United States and not much higher in Europe, and in which resources are underemployed generally, then it seems to me that the problem in your framework is excess world savings.

*Corden*: The model I have in mind assumes that employment depends on demand, as I think we're implying here in the short run at least, and that unemployment should be dealt with by appropriate monetary policy in each country.

*Cooper*: Why not monetary *and* fiscal policy in each country?

*Corden*: I would rely on monetary policy, because we want budget deficits to be as low as possible, subject to all the structural considerations, so as to make funds available for the developing countries.

*Kaldor*: Would you disagree with the proposition that, for one reason or another, Keynesian policies are not now successfully pursued—in the sense that there is a lot of involuntary unemployment—and that attempts to stimulate savings will not increase the volume of savings but will simply further reduce the volume of employment and production?

*Corden*: In one sense, of course, Keynesian policies are not successfully pursued—in the sense, as you point out, that we have involuntary unemployment. Keynesian demand expansion, I think, would reduce the unemployment in the short run, and in that sense

Keynesian policies are not now successfully pursued. But, in another sense, they *are* successfully pursued. The authorities—I mean the central banks and governments—have made a decision, rightly or wrongly, to have a trade-off between inflation and unemployment. I'm not saying that they're precisely where they want to be, but to some extent they've got the unemployment they wanted, presumably, and they've got the reduction in inflation they wanted. So, in that sense, we have to say the demand policies are more or less successfully pursued. If they are not, I would remedy this by more monetary expansion. So I'm not completely disagreeing with Lord Kaldor.

*Cooper*: We're going to come back to this topic a little more systematically later. I'd like to turn now to Professor Schröder, who has been patiently waiting for a long time.

*Schröder*: Let me raise a basic question. I wonder whether there is a connection between the level of the real interest rate in the world and the huge amount of international debt. I would argue that this debt has raised the real interest rate. If it is true that the larger the international debt, the higher the real interest rate, then I think it would be wise to ask why we have such a huge international debt. One reason, undoubtedly, is the drastic increase in the price of oil. But another reason for the large debt, I think, is the willingness of governments, as in the case of Germany, to offer guarantees, for political reasons, when private banks make loans to foreign governments. The question then is whether that is a good thing in the long run, because capital goes in a direction that it would not go in the absence of government interference.

*Cooper*: Following on that, I would raise a question which I don't know the answer to, but maybe somebody else here does. I think it is valid to look at borrowing not just by the U.S. government but by governments worldwide. But one also has to look at lending by governments worldwide. And until 1982, of course, the OPEC countries were doing a lot of lending. If one consolidated the government accounts of the world, so to speak, as of let's say 1981, when real interest rates were very high, how does that situation compare with, say, 1973 or 1977? I don't know the answer to this question, but it seems to me an interesting, researchable topic whether the government net call on real resources was greater, relative to gross world product, in 1981 than in 1977 or in 1973.

*Heller*: Well, take the U.S. budget deficit of $200 billion.

*Cooper*: No, in 1981, when the OPEC surplus was big, the U.S. budget deficit was $70 billion, or something like that.

*Heller*: Okay, but if you take 1983 you're talking about a global budget deficit of around $500 billion. That is clearly at a time when the OPEC surplus has disappeared.

*Cooper*: And also private investment has virtually disappeared.

*Heller*: Oh, yes; so whatever the argument may have been in 1981, it's certainly out the window in 1983.

*Cooper*: But we've been in the depths of a recession. The question is whether, extracting from cyclical factors, the government claim on the world output of goods and services is higher now than, say, ten years ago. I took that to be the form of the question. I call now on Dr. Podbielski.

*Gisele Podbielski*: I want to say a few words about Italy—first of all, because we are in Italy; secondly, because most of the people here have illustrated their arguments with references to the United States; thirdly, because all the problems of economic recovery are more extreme, more exacerbated, in Italy; and, fourthly, because Italy is, *par excellence*, an illustration of deep-seated structural problems—problems which more urgently require attention than our serious short-term problems.

Let me give you a few facts to show how serious the situation is. Despite considerable efforts to deal with the problem, we still have a rate of inflation of about 16 percent. The government budget deficit amounts to 15 percent of the gross domestic product, which is about the highest percentage anywhere; the average for other industrial countries is 3 to 4 percent. Labor costs show great rigidity despite— or because of—our sliding-scale mechanism. Our built-in rigidities and constraints make it very difficult to relax monetary restrictions. In spite of stagnating domestic investment, borrowing from abroad has been extremely high; Mr. Ciampi, the governor of our central bank, has said that Italy is "drowning" in debt. There is an official estimate that if the growth rate were to rise to 1.5 percent instead of 1 percent, the rate of inflation would rise to 20 percent, with hardly any addition to industrial employment.

Now, with respect to structural problems, let me quickly mention what everyone here knows—that Italy is a divided country, a dual economy, where we have, in the south, a very large underdeveloped section in an otherwise advanced industrialized country. We have another dualism—a state-subsidized sector which includes steel, shipbuilding, petrochemicals, and energy, as against a private large-company sector which is just beginning to recover. We have a rather successful small private sector, which is constantly being mentioned as being inventive and thriving. In southern Italy, we have the problem of competition with the developing countries and, in the advanced industrial sectors, the problem of competition with other industrial countries. There is also the problem of Mediterranean agriculture, which is very badly protected by Common Market agricultural policy.

Now there is great concern that if, through government policies, we were to succeed in stimulating investment, the effect of the new investment might be largely labor-saving and modernizing, without any contribution to the problem of unemployment. I think this is a rather wide problem, not limited to the Italian scene. But, in your discussion of monetary policies, interest rates, fiscal policies, payments mechanisms, and so on, I hope you will bear in mind to what extent your proposals apply to these particular structural problems, which, while they assume an extreme form in Italy, are by no means confined to Italy.

*Cooper*: If I understood you correctly, you made the rather dramatic statement that a ½ percent increase in the growth rate would lead to an increase of 4 percentage points in the inflation rate, with no increase in employment. Is that independent of the source of demand? Does it make a difference, for example, whether the increased demand is in the form of additional export orders or in the form of additional government purchases?

*Podbielski*: These are very relevant questions; I was simply citing the conclusions of a public report.

*Magnifico*: No, the inflation rate is not independent of the source of demand.

*Cooper*: So it's not independent.

*Magnifico*: It rests on alternative assumptions concerning the public sector. Unless public expenditures are cut, inflation will be higher; if they are cut, then we will have lower inflation but also lower growth, or even negative growth. This year, for example, we expect a growth rate of between 3 percent and minus 1 percent.

But let me add some qualifications regarding inflation. There is a very wide gap between the Italian consumer-price index, which includes rents and public utilities, and the wholesale-price index. We are in the process of decontrolling rent, and we are also adjusting upward the public-utility rates charged to consumers. These price adjustments of course affect the consumer-price index, and are really a response to repressed inflation rather than to current inflationary stimuli. Thus, in sharp contrast to the double-digit rise in the consumer-price index, the wholesale-price index in recent months has been going up very slowly; the latest figure is only .3 percent.

*Cooper*: Per month?

*Magnifico*: Per month.

*Cooper*: So about 3 to 4 percent a year.

*Magnifico*: The figures for the last three months were .4 , .5, and .3 percent. But I think the government deficit is still too high. The problem in Italy is not just the size, but the composition, of the deficit. When we look at what we are getting for it, we find that we are getting very little.

*Arndt*: I'd like to say a word about inflation from another angle. When countries, as a result of anti-inflationary policies, slide down their Phillips Curves faster than they had expected—having focused on reducing inflation and thereby getting more unemployment than they had bargained for—they are likely to be strongly tempted to resort to protectionist measures as a short-term expedient. But such devices impede a country's long-term adjustment capacity and, once put into effect, are very difficult for an individual country, acting unilaterally, to remove. I would argue that this may be the most important area for international economic coordination, both in avoiding greater protectionism and in reducing existing trade barriers.

*Mundell*: Since both Max Corden and Sven Arndt have referred to the Phillips Curve, I think it would be a mistake for me not to comment on that. In Australia, perhaps, and also in Britain, the general monetarist approach has been to try to stop inflation by increasing the level of unemployment, the assumption being that there exists a large Phillips Curve trade-off. But the experiment that's been the heart of Reaganomics, or at least the supply-side part of Reaganomics, has been, not to move along the Phillips Curve, but to *shift* it. And the way to shift it is to use the fiscal and monetary mix that we discussed in this room twelve years ago—namely, tax cuts combined with tight money.

I wouldn't want to defend Reaganomics, because the mistakes of Reaganomics have led to a higher level of unemployment than anybody wanted. The monetarists in the administration wanted a recession; they wanted to increase the unemployment rate, because they saw that as the principal way in which they could deal with inflationary wage claims. This policy did stop the inflation, but it stopped it with an unnecessarily large increase in unemployment. The correct approach has now been in effect only since the second half of last year [1982]; when the second round of tax cuts went into effect, then the economy started to shoot up. Since then, the unemployment rate has begun to fall, while the inflation rate has continued to come down.

That's the policy we need to push for, but I am afraid that the recovery will be aborted unless the policy is pursued more vigorously. And we should note that the United States has not moved along the Phillips Curve; it has shifted the curve despite the administration's errors and the stupidity of those errors. It has shifted the curve dramatically downward and to the left, proving that the Phillips Curve is not something fixed and rigid that people have to accept, but that, with intelligent policy, it can be shifted through an appropriate policy mix.

*Kaldor*: May I ask a question? You said that America has falling inflation rates, falling interest rates, and now falling unemployment rates. This seems to me success. To what do you attribute that? Is it a series of accidents or the work of some very clever people who planned it all?

*Mundell*: Well, unfortunately, you weren't at the 1971 Bologna conference, where we discussed these matters at great length. It's all printed in a book which Randall Hinshaw edited.* I don't think we should repeat all that discussion here; the people who were around this table in 1971 would be bored sick with it, so if Randall would give you a copy of the book, you can read the whole dialogue.

But just let me say a word about the Reagan program. The fact is that the policy mix I advocated only got started in the middle of last year. There was a two-year delay in effectively implementing the tax cuts, but we have since had this tremendous success. The delay was of some embarrassment to me, because in 1980, in the middle of the election campaign, I made a speech in New York predicting that if the program advocated by the Reagan economic team were put through, the Dow-Jones average would hit 1100 and might even hit 1200. Well, the program was delayed for two years, and the Dow-Jones average didn't hit those figures until two years after my prediction. The theory was right, but the monetarists, led by Milton Friedman, Beryl Sprinkel, and whoever else you want to blame, were against it.

*Cooper*: I now have requests for two-handed comments from three people: Howard Craven, Max Corden, and Bob Heller. Before they come in, though, I would like to point out that Bob Mundell, in

*Randall Hinshaw, ed., *Inflation as a Global Problem* (Baltimore: Johns Hopkins University Press, 1972).

his reference to tax cuts and to the Tax Act of 1981, emphasized the supply-side effects. The Tax Act did have supply-side effects, but it also had demand-increasing effects, and his conclusions on the delay in the tax cuts really apply to the demand-increasing effects, not to the supply-side effects. The supply-side effects come into play at once, if not before, the tax cuts actually take place. Indeed, on supply-side grounds, people should have already anticipated a year ago the tax reduction of July 1983. So while I would agree with much of what Bob has said, I would substitute the words "demand-increasing" for "supply-side."

*Mundell*: Just let me say with two hands that I am a two-handed economist; I believe in both demand and supply—that both blades of the scissors do the cutting—but that at different times we need to stress one, the other, or both. Prior to 1979, I emphasized the supply side, because inflation was shooting up toward 20 percent, and I thought that was the major issue. But as unemployment increased up toward 11 percent, I became again, as is my normal custom, both a supply-side and a demand-side economist. And when both sides work to reinforce each other, we get success, which is exactly what we've had since last August.

*Cooper*: My point was a narrow one—that the supply-side effects were not delayed for two years; it was the demand effects that were delayed.

*Craven*: Well, I have a problem on the timing too, but of a different nature. The tax cuts, to the extent that they were stimulating consumption expenditures, did not delay matters until August, because in the second quarter of 1982 real personal consumption expenditures reached an all-time high. And since that time, there have been successive highs in every quarter. So there was no delay in the recovery of personal consumption expenditure.

*Heller*: Nominal or real?

*Craven*: Both.

*Mundell*: But not counting growth; there has been no growth. In order to keep the unemployment rate down, you have to keep the economy growing.

*Craven*: But consumption expenditures have been reaching new highs in each quarter during the past year.

*Mundell*: Yes, but they must grow at a rate which takes account of normal accumulation and of the growth of the labor force.

*Craven*: Well, if you were to assume that the prior rate of growth of consumption expenditures was a normal rate—the rate you had, say, in the first quarter of 1981, when the Reagan administration took over—you surely would not expect the recent abnormally high rate of growth to continue.

*Cooper*: This can be carried on over tea. Did you have another point?

*Craven*: Yes; my second point is on business expansion. The tax cuts did not show any sort of response on business fixed investment until the first quarter of this year. And that response is still very weak. Capacity utilization is still very low—still not high enough to make new investment very attractive. But there has been another element in the economic recovery, and that has been the continued strong increase in government spending, both in nominal and in real terms.

*Corden*: I think we're all in favor of tax cuts, looked at in isolation, either because of their incentive effects or, in the case of Europe, because they may reduce wage demands. But the question in my mind is: Are we assuming that tax cuts will generate so much extra income that total tax revenue, allowing a little time, will not fall? If it does fall, we will have to look at the interest-rate effect again. We can't ignore that aspect, and I personally feel that the U.S. budget deficit, present and prospective, is one of the biggest problems facing the world. And the tax cuts are part of that problem.

*Cooper*: Max, would you have made the same statement one year ago or two years ago? This is a serious question, because what you've just said has now become the conventional wisdom in the financial community and the financial press—that the U.S. budget deficit is one of the most serious problems in the world today. I actually find myself coming to share that view now, because, on current trajectories, the deficit is getting bigger year by year. But the thing that troubles me is that the financial press was saying the same thing one year ago, and, in my analytical judgment, the 1982 budget deficit was no problem whatsoever in terms of all the things we've been talking about. It was not disproportionate, given the state of the economy. But would you have held your present view one year ago—or two years ago, as many financial correspondents did?

*Corden*: One year ago, I did have this view; I can't remember about two years ago. But the U.S. budget deficit as a percentage of GNP is going to be no higher than in the case of a number of other countries, such as Japan and, I think, maybe even Germany.

*Cooper*: But the percentage in the United States is growing.

*Corden*: The problem is that when such a large economy as the United States decides to join the other countries having large budget deficits, that has a big impact on the world capital market. That's the bit that worries me. And I'm also thinking of the effects on the developing countries and of the need to keep interest rates down for their sake.

*Kaldor*: Why do you assume that a higher deficit leads to higher interest rates?

*Corden*: Because the money has to be borrowed.

*Kaldor*: Well, it can be supplied.

*Corden*: Printed?

*Kaldor*: Printed. We financed World War II at a 2 percent interest rate, and the budget deficit in relation to GNP, both in England and in America, was much higher than it is now. That did no real harm. There is no evidence that a 15 percent interest rate calls forth extra saving to finance the budget deficit as compared to a low interest rate, nor is there any evidence that at a high interest rate the economy is in a better situation, given the same budget deficit, than at a low interest rate. These are old prejudices.

*Heller*: My point has to do with Bob Mundell. The U.S. tax cut should have been implemented a lot earlier. Furthermore, instead of being in stages, it should have been front-loaded. In 1981, the United States was still reasonably close to full employment of labor and of plant capacity. Thus the tax cut at that time would have resulted in the traditional supply-side effect—increased tax collection—as contrasted with the present situation, in which the tax cuts have fallen largely on barren ground, especially in the investment area, where there is underutilized capacity all around. But I don't think the debate between the supply-siders and the monetarists is fully decided by the recent upturn in U.S. economic activity, because the money-supply growth began to accelerate at about the same time that Mundell was talking about. The monetarists, although they decry the sharp increase in money-supply growth that we have now—around 15 percent—say that much of the pickup in economic activity that we presently observe is due to monetary expansion.

*Mundell*: I have a quick answer to that. The monetarists cannot take credit for the upturn, because, according to monetarist theory, there is a long lag between the increase in the rate of monetary expansion and the increase in industrial output—a lag of between nine and eighteen months. So you can't say that the increase in the money supply has caused the expansion in economic activity; you have to argue that the expansion has drawn in the money supply through an accommodating Federal Reserve policy.

*Heller*: With the chairman's indulgence, may I say that I think Mundell has read his Friedman wrong. It's a short lag between money changes and output changes—three to six months—and a long lag between money changes and price-level changes.

*Mundell*: Bob, I didn't read it; I listened to it in Chicago for seven or eight years.

*Cooper*: That sounds like another good topic for tea. Dr. Emminger wants to comment.

*Emminger*: Just two brief remarks on this discussion. First, the comparison was made between the budget deficit of the United States and that of other industrial countries. As a percentage of GNP, the American budget deficit up to last year was lower than, for instance, in Germany or in Japan. But when the deficit is measured as a percentage of the total net savings of the economy, the figure for the United States, as I mentioned this morning, was over 70 percent, whereas in Japan it was 20 percent and in Germany—Mr. Matthes may correct me if I'm wrong—it was between one-third . . .

*Matthes [interrupting]*: One-third.

*Emminger*: One third of total net savings. And that's a very big difference. The second difference—and I'm surprised that this has not been mentioned up to now—is the structure of the deficit. In Germany, for instance, we have a budget deficit of which less than half seems to be structural. But in the United States, according to the latest *Economic Report of the President*, which I have read very carefully, the larger part of the deficit is structural. In particular, the deficit which has been produced by the tax cuts is a structural thing, which will not disappear through an upturn in the economy. And the same is true of the increase in defense expenditure. So the two major reasons for the very large increase in the U.S. budget deficit are of a structural nature, and they will not disappear with the recovery.

*Cooper*: May I just comment on that? I think you have to date those statements very carefully. I don't know what the president's *Economic Report* says; my judgment is that for this year, with an estimated budget deficit of $200 billion, about one-third—the same fraction as in Germany—is structural. The difference is that the structural component in the American projections has a big impact on the world capital market. That's the bit that worries me. I'm thinking primarily of the effects on the developing countries and of the need in that connection to keep interest rates down.

*Corden*: I'd like to come back to a comment by Lord Kaldor that I wasn't able to answer. I've now thought of the answer. I'm absolutely determined that we're going to get something that he and I agree on, and this is it, probably. Let us agree first of all, just to set out the precise assumptions, that there has been a lack of aggregate demand in the United States, with excess capacity and unemployment. Now that situation requires an increase in nominal demand brought about by monetary or fiscal policy.

*Kaldor*: Real demand, I would say, not nominal demand.

*Corden*: Well, an increase in nominal demand would lead to an increase in real demand; I assume that inflation would not prevent this. My argument is simply that, for any given increase in demand that needs to be brought about, it is desirable from a world point of view that it should be brought about with low interest rates rather than with high interest rates. And therefore I would have preferred monetary expansion rather than fiscal expansion.

*Kaldor*: I don't disagree on that.

Giovanni Magnifico
and Members of the
Conference

# The Problem of Third World Debt

*Chairman Cooper*: I propose that we devote the rest of this afternoon to the problem of external debt. How important is Third World debt from a global point of view? Is it a serious barrier to recovery or not? If it is, what, if anything, can or should be done about it? Giovanni Magnifico touched on these matters briefly this morning, and I am asking him now to elaborate.

*Magnifico*: I think I agree with you, Mr. Chairman, that we are not at the present time dealing with a global problem; it is rather a problem of a dozen or so countries. It might become a global problem if not properly dealt with; there could be a chain reaction, a sort of domino effect, with dire results for the banking, credit, and financial structures of the world. Now that is clearly the thing to avoid, and the danger in this connection is that a large chunk of the international debt is short term. It cannot be paid as originally scheduled; it must be refinanced.

The debt problem arose, of course, from the oil crises of the 1970s. The banks came to the rescue—the banks are always the first to be asked—but what is now needed is a smaller role for the banking system, with a more active role for the nonbanking sectors of the international capital market. The problem is to place with the nonbanking sector the debt to the banks of the financially pressed developing countries. Industrial countries are already doing this; Italy, for example, is issuing bonds on the international capital market, thus replacing part of its short-term and medium-term debt to the banking system. But the LDCs cannot do this. Anyone who has had anything to do with the international capital market knows that the developing countries would encounter immense difficulties in issuing bonds for placement with private investors, institutional investors, or other nonbanking investors.

What is needed is the intermediation of an official institution. I think the World Bank is the institution best suited for this role because of its long experience both with the long-term capital market and with the problems of the developing countries. So the proposal which I put forward last October [1982] at the *Financial Times* conference in London was that the World Bank issue bonds—special bonds—the proceeds of which would be used to grant long-term loans to LDC debtor countries, which would use the funds to repay their short-term debt to the banking system. The loans to LDCs would be on a case-by-case basis. The plan would be worked out in cooperation with the International Monetary Fund, the Fund providing finance for countries which find it very difficult to finance their current-account deficits, whereas the World Bank would provide finance for the consolidation of the LDC debt.

Of course I realize that there are problems with such an arrangement. For example, the World Bank might be worried that the scheme would jeopardize its triple-A rating. There would be ways, however, to avoid this danger. One possibility would be the creation of a debt-consolidation account, which would be separated from the World Bank as such, but would be managed by the World Bank and thus use the Bank's know-how. But it would have its own balance sheet.

Numerous benefits might result from such an operation. For one thing, the banks would become more efficient. Because of the debt crisis, the banks have seen a considerable part of their presumably liquid assets, in effect, frozen; when banks receive telexes from the IMF, from Treasury ministers, from central bank governors asking them not to reduce lines of credit, or to restore them back to where they were at certain dates, those banks cannot help feeling that such assets are in fact not liquid. This situation of course makes the banks much more cautious, much more risk-averse. Banks should be risk-averse, but not too much so. Under my proposal, however, much of this debt would be shifted to the longer-term end of the market, which would take some of the pressure off short-term interest rates, as well as medium-term rates, which are indexed to the short-term rates. Incidentally, I think that short-term interest rates *are* an important determinant of long-term rates. In any case, the proposed arrangement, by reducing the pressure on bank credit, would tend to bring down short-term interest rates, and this would be helpful both for the LDCs and for the rest of the world.

There is much more that I could add to what I have said, but this is basically the sort of thing which I think could help us get out of our present difficulties.

*Cooper*: May I ask a question of clarification? The World Bank now has its structural-adjustment lending, which is not keyed to par-

ticular projects, as traditional World Bank lending is, but rather to
changes in policy—typically, though not always, in conjunction with
the International Monetary Fund. In other words, the lending is for
general balance-of-payments support, but is conditioned on policy
changes. How does your proposal differ from what the World Bank is
doing, except possibly in scale?

*Magnifico*: Well, it differs in scale without the word *possibly*. I
think that for the World Bank to play a significant role in the international debt problem, it should double the scale of its operations.
The structural lending program of the World Bank is essentially lending for the current-account balance of payments.

*Cooper*: But it's generalized support.

*Magnifico*: There should be stronger links with the IMF. A country should be able to come to a committee made up of the IMF and
the World Bank to discuss its need for not having to cut imports by
more than a certain amount, its needs for certain special projects, and
its international debt problems—particularly the short-term component. Following this discussion or examination or negotiation, the
country might be entitled to receive financial assistance to be used
for meeting its short-term, or part of its short-term, debt.

*Jamison*: As I understand your proposal, its essence is to substitute long-term loans for short-term loans. I am wondering whether
your purpose is simply to postpone the inevitable. Does your proposal
provide for amortized payments over a period of years, or does the
principal become due twenty years from now instead of next year? I
also wonder whether the funds would be available only to those
countries that would be able to repay in full over the long term. If
that is the case, then your proposal doesn't deal with the most threat-
ening segment of the international debt structure, which is the debt
of countries whose prospects for repayment are dubious. That's where
the real problem lies.

*Cooper*: Before Giovanni responds, perhaps we should hear some
more comments. Nicky wants to say something.

*Kaldor*: Well, I see this very largely, though not entirely, as a
bookkeeping transaction which enables banks that are in the unhappy
position of having assets which they ought to write off as bad debts—
but can't without becoming insolvent or bankrupt—to substitute in
their books obligations of the World Bank for their loans to Mexico,
Argentina, and the like. Obviously, this would solve the problem of
the banking system, but whether it's the best solution is another
question. I would prefer a solution along the lines which the Bank of
England has followed in the past—namely, the so-called life-

boat, in which a levy is imposed on all banks in order to prevent the insolvency of those banks which have got themselves into a difficult situation. This approach could be combined with a big reduction in the interest rate for the developing countries, because high interest rates are a very large part of the problem. But otherwise I don't see anything unique in your proposal; in the end, banks will simply hold one piece of paper instead of another piece of paper.

*Magnifico*: No, no, that's not true, because I am proposing that the piece of paper be sold to the nonbanking sector of the capital market.

*Kaldor*: That is on the assumption that the paper would be taken up outside the banking sector.

*Magnifico*: Well, yes; that's fundamental.

*Kaldor*: This reminds one very much of the Group of Twenty recommendation to substitute for the official dollar balances the so-called substitution accounts in the IMF.

*Cooper*: I now have a number of requests for the floor, all of which have been billed as two-handed statements. Bob Heller is first.

*Heller*: I'd like to get Giovanni's reaction to a proposal reasonably similar to his own, but with an important difference. One of my colleagues thinks that it would be very difficult to sell the necessary volume of new World Bank bonds to the public; the World Bank is already the biggest borrower in the international capital market, so it would have a very hard selling job to do. But the banks are very good at gathering assets from the nonbank public, so why not have the banks, as the gatherers of the deposits, lend those funds to the World Bank, and then proceed exactly Giovanni's way.

*Emminger*: I think this is all very premature. There are two problems at the present time. The first is that, at least in a number of cases, great effort is required to maintain the existing credit lines of the banking system. This problem has been made more difficult by recent remarks by Mr. Leutwiler, president of the Swiss National Bank and head of the Bank for International Settlements in Basel. Two or three weeks ago in London, he indicated that he considered it to be inappropriate for central banks to exert pressure on the commercial banks to maintain existing credit lines. I know that, on the basis of these remarks, some of our banks—not the major ones, but the middle-sized banks—have announced that they will no longer renew their short-term lending. The result has been that the major banks have had to take over the share of these smaller banks.

The second difficulty is that it is not sufficient merely to maintain the existing credit lines; additional bank credit is needed. In the case of Mexico and Brazil, for example, the International Monetary Fund has been pressuring the banks not only to reschedule the existing loans but to provide additional loans amounting, I think, to 7 or 8 percent of their outstanding loan totals. This will be a difficult job. A few months ago, a good friend of mine whom you all know, Arthur Burns, who is now American ambassador in Bonn, said in an interview in the German press that formerly we had to criticize the banks for being so foolish in extending such extravagant loans, but that now we have to pray that they will continue to be so foolish!

Finally, a word on this very interesting proposal by Giovanni Magnifico about debt consolidation, with possible guarantees by governments. The latter, of course, is a feature which is contained in a number of other such proposals—that, somehow or other, governments or central banks should give guarantees or should contribute in some way. Up to now, I have not seen a single proposal which, in my view, would not involve new legislation for such bailing-out operations. And when I look at the United States, where the Congress has shown such hostility toward anything that looks like a bailing out of the banks, I just do not see any practical possibility for such a plan. Maybe in a very big crisis—that's a different thing. If we have a real breakdown, then, of course, everybody will hasten to cooperate. But not before that.

*Gutowski*: My questions reflect the same concerns as those just expressed by Dr. Emminger. First, Giovanni, does your scheme depend on guarantees by governments of the highly industrialized countries? Second, is it a plan to bail out the developing countries, or is it a plan to bail out the banks? I have the feeling that it's the second, because if the developing countries have only a liquidity problem, then, without your scheme, the banks are forced to get together to reschedule the debt and to extend the repayment period. On the other hand, if the developing countries have a solvency problem because they have used credit for consumption or for unsound investments, then your proposal is not a solution but just a postponement of the problem, as Mr. Jamison said. So my question is: Do you simply want to bail out the banks? I am not opposed to that, but what is the price that the banks have to pay for this service? They will be happy to be bailed out. It should be made clear, however, that this is a once-and-for-all exercise; if that is not said, the banks may feel free to lend again in the same way, and may expect to be bailed out every seven years or so, as in the Bible.

*Corden*: The point I was about to make has just been made by Armin. The basic question is: Are we dealing with an LDC liquidity problem or with an LDC solvency problem? My impression with regard to the three major Latin American countries in debt is that the problem may be mainly one of liquidity. If so, the solution is some kind of consolidation involving the conversion of short-term into long-term debt. If we are dealing with a solvency problem, then the solution becomes more difficult, doesn't it? The solvency issue really boils down to which taxpayers are going to pay in the end.

On the practical issue of Giovanni's proposal, like Dr. Emminger, I just can't see the U.S. Congress agreeing to anything like that. However desirable it might be, I can't see the Congress agreeing to the World Bank being permitted to borrow on such a scale, with the implicit guarantees by the countries that own the Bank. This is the practical problem.

*Arndt*: My comments run along the same lines—whether or not we're talking about a bail-out, whether we're talking about a liquidity or solvency issue. To what extent would we be bailing out mainly banks? To what extent would we be bailing out mainly countries? And if Giovanni's proposal were to become a permanent fixture, what would that do to the incentives that both banks and countries will have in the future?

*Mundell*: I would like to ask Max Corden to tell us the difference, for a country, between a liquidity problem and a solvency problem.

*Corden*: What do I mean?

*Mundell*: In the context of countries, not firms. How do we know whether Mexico's problem or Brazil's problem is a liquidity problem or a solvency problem?

*Corden*: Well, of course, one never knows until after the event, but what I have in mind is that, taking a long view, do we think that if we converted these loans into long-term obligations, Mexico or Brazil would be able to pay the interest on them? If we do, then I would say it's purely a liquidity problem. But if we think, really, that these countries are going to be continuously in trouble—that they won't be able to pay the interest—then we have a solvency problem.

*Magnifico*: Yes, but whether Mexico or Brazil will be able to pay the interest will depend on what happens to the world economy, what happens to international trade, what happens to the price of oil. It will depend on many things, so there is no easy answer to Bob's question.

*Mundell*: I would simply say that if you solve any country's—or, in fact, anybody's—liquidity problem, you would never have a solvency problem.

*Corden*: Yes, but let me elaborate my answer to that. What I had in mind was that we've been through a bad recession, coupled with very high interest rates, and that all this was basically unexpected. It's at least possible that these conditions may go away in due course; that would surely make a significant difference to this kind of problem. I don't know all the details of each of the countries, and presumably one has to look at each country separately, but the question in my mind is whether, once world conditions have improved, the whole thing will look quite different. If so, then I'd say we were dealing with a liquidity problem; it's just a matter of tiding over a few years. But if the borrowing continues to be madly out of line—and I think that may be true of some African countries—then we are in a different ball game.

*Gutowski*: I just want to say to Bob Mundell that I consider a solvency problem to exist if a country cannot resume a reasonable growth path of its gross domestic product—its GDP—and therefore will be unable to repay all of its debt.

*Cooper*: With world economic conditions being different from what they are now?

*Gutowski*: Yes, of course; that's right.

*Triffin*: In thinking about this issue, we should remember that, from a strictly economic point of view, as long as a country is in current-account deficit, it will not repay in real terms; it cannot repay *really*. And as long as a creditor country is in current-account surplus, it will not—in real terms—get repaid. This simple economic truth seems to be totally ignored or forgotten when we discuss the political and legal aspects of international debt.

Giovanni did not mention the subject of maturities—whether repayment, in nominal terms, would be by installments or at a fixed date. I am wondering whether he has considered the possibility that the loans extended under his plan might be in the form, very prestigious in former times, of consols—that is to say, interest-bearing obligations without a maturity date but redeemable at the debtor country's option.

*Scharrer*: Professor Triffin has just made a most interesting suggestion, but why do we need an international organization to deal with this matter? Why don't the banks just go to Mexico or Brazil or Argentina, and say, "Look, we have this short-term claim on your country which is now due; we are prepared to extend this into an indefinite loan of the consol variety or into a fifty-year loan, so please give us the paper on it." If the banks did not want to hold the paper, they could sell it, though perhaps at a big discount. The discount would be the penalty the banks would have to pay in order to get out from under the original short-term loans. But we don't need an international organization to accomplish this.

*Cooper*: We'll give Giovanni a chance to try to deal with all these questions, and then I'll have the last word on the subject.

*Magnifico*: Well, it looks as if my proposal has already been buried, and I doubt whether I can perform a miracle. But let me try.

I think the first question raised was by Mr. Jamison on the matter of reimbursement. I omitted any details on that, but I assumed that the loans by the World Bank to the LDCs would be amortized in a normal manner, with perhaps an initial grace period of two, three, or five years. Robert Heller said that the banks are very good at collecting savings from the public; why should they not funnel some of these savings to the World Bank? But this is exactly what leads to the over-expansion of the bank mediation function that has caused our present difficulties. I think we should try to do without the banks now and transfer the LDC debt to the nonbanking sector.

*Kaldor*: But the nonbanking sector must be willing to absorb this paper, and I don't think it is.

*Magnifico*: Well, Dr. Scharrer put his finger on the issue; there will always be a price which will make it possible to sell or buy something. Therefore, the real issue is whether you want to do it at any price—whether you want the banks to take the entire loss or whether it would be better, in the interest of all parties concerned, to divide the losses between the banks and, ultimately, the taxpayers. In other words, the question is whether the matter should be resolved through the market mechanism or whether, because of the inability of the debtor countries to repay, taxpayers in the more affluent countries should put up some of the money to make good a part of these losses. But what I am saying is that if we are able to spread over a longer period of time the liabilities of these countries, there is a better chance that those countries will be able to repay—particularly if their policies are supervised by the International Monetary Fund.

*Kaldor*: You haven't answered one point of mine. How do you view what I call the lifeboat principle, under which the Bank of England made a levy on all the banks for the purpose of assisting those banks that otherwise would have become insolvent?

*Magnifico*: I would favor the insurance principle, but that would have to be in operation before a crisis develops. The most important thing to decide is whether we want to discuss anything of this kind and, if so, then decide what sort of penalty system would be best.

The decision to make is whether we want to envisage, in principle, something of this kind or not. If the answer is yes, then we can see how we should organize it—particularly from the very important point of view of who should pay.

*Emminger*: But don't all these plans need legislation?

*Magnifico*: They would need legislation. If I understood you correctly, you did not make much of a distinction between government money and central bank money—at least in your reporting of other people's views. I think it makes a great difference. If there are losses and somebody has to be bailed out, this should be done with government money, not with central bank money. What is happening now is wrong; the bailing out is being done with the funds of central banks and of the IMF.

*Emminger*: No, no; in the American case, it will be the government that will have to provide the finance for the increase in IMF quotas. So it is government money that is at stake, and the Congress is very hostile to using government money for bailing out banks. That was my point. Unless there is a very big crisis, I don't believe that governments will obtain the legislation that is necessary for them to take part in such plans.

*Magnifico*: Well, Dr. Emminger, there are some central banks which have lent money.

*Emminger*: I am not speaking about central banks; I am speaking about governments. My point was that government money and government guarantees cannot be put into operation except on the basis of new legislation.

*Magnifico*: I agree with you.

*Emminger*: And it is practically impossible to get this legislation.

*Magnifico*: Unless we create a favorable climate of informed opinion. Then, in the end, governments might do it.

*Kaldor*: That's right; that's what happened in England, very successfully, and I don't see why it can't happen again.

*Cooper*: I'm afraid I agree with Dr. Emminger on this as a practical matter. I take this problem seriously. It hangs as a dark cloud over the recovery, because it creates the kind of investment uncertainty that Dr. Scharrer earlier spoke of as also applying to protection. These debtor countries now have become major markets—not decisive for the recovery of the industrial countries but nonetheless major markets. Under the force of circumstances, they are retrenching in order to continue servicing their debts. That's a major negative for the world economy. And the possibility that one or another of them might not make it, thereby triggering a series of defaults, is one of the major sources of uncertainty now.

I have no doubt that if we could wave one of those magic wands that appear in children's fairy stories, and thereby add five years to the maturity of all the debt of the developing countries, both creditors and debtors would be better off in the present circumstances. My problem is that I don't see any way to get from here to there. Peter Kenen has put forward a proposal very similar to Magnifico's scheme, but with the explicit feature that it would penalize the banks. He would have the banks discount their paper with a new institution at a suggested penalty rate of 10 percent. In other words, the institution would pay only ninety cents on the dollar to the banks, but would make it possible for the banks to get out from under the debt on these terms.

But all such schemes involve government financing or, at a minimum, government guarantees. Thus they all involve new legislation. I can't speak for other legislative bodies, and perhaps I'm unduly influenced by the battle scars I still carry from dealing with the U.S. Congress, but the process of trying to get any such legislation, at least in the U.S. case, would be prolonged and painful. In the meantime, the banks would stop the lending they need to do, because they would wait for the legislative situation to clarify. Since I agree with Dr. Emminger that it would be necessary not only to roll over the existing debt but to add to that debt, the process of trying to get a preferred solution would, I think, actually be perverse in its effects by creating legislative uncertainty for many months while the process was going on.

So I somewhat pessimistically conclude that the best path is the one we're on, and that is piecemeal rescheduling. But we must recognize the facts of life—that there's going to be a lot of rescheduling in the months ahead. One very modest improvement that could be made in that process would be to take three years of debt at a time, instead of just one. The convention at present is to take the debt coming due in the year ahead and to reschedule that, with, say, a three-year grace period and then seven years to pay—something like that. And I think in present circumstances one could perhaps take, not a long-term view, but a medium-term view, with the aim of stretching out the maturities.

*Kaldor*: What about interest?

*Cooper*: The interest rate would continue to be the market rate of interest. One perhaps need not be in favor of those very heavy re-

scheduling premiums that offend Bob Mundell, but the interest rate
would continue to be the market rate.

*Kaldor*: You have a situation like Mexico, where I understand
that interest payments account for the entire current-account deficit.

*Cooper*: Well, that's true of Brazil and probably true of Mexico
too. I think a precondition for getting out of this problem is a steady
recovery. Without such a recovery, I think the problem will move
from being a manageable problem to an unmanageable problem
within two years, by which I mean there will be major defaults and
all the consequences that flow from that. But we come back to Max
Corden's distinction; if the world economic environment is improving, there is nothing wrong with new lending to cover interest payments during a transitional period. It's only over a long period that
borrowing to pay interest makes no sense. But I fear the legislative
process; not only would it be difficult but it would actually be perverse in its effects, because the banks would stop lending while it
was taking place. That's my problem with all such schemes, however
imaginatively put forward.

*Scharrer*: Why, in the Kenen proposal, is there a 10 percent discount?

*Cooper*: It's arbitrary.

*Scharrer*: But we have a mechanism to figure out the discount on
the loans which are pending; we can use the market.

*Cooper*: Well, Kenen's proposal is not a market proposal. It involves guarantees and interest subsidies. Under a market solution,
I'm afraid the discounts on these loans would be extremely heavy,
given the myopia of markets, and we might well precipitate what
we're trying to avoid—namely, the insolvency of some of the banks.
We do have a measure of market effects in Mexico, which, after all,
was formerly a very successful floater of bonds. They are trading at
very heavy discounts now.

Unless there are other comments on this topic, we're at the end
of the day. What I would like us to do tomorrow is to turn to other
problems relating to global recovery. With your indulgence, let me
just take a minute or two to provoke you with my own views, without offering at this point a full rationale for them.

I am in the present context an expansionist. And I am a coordinated expansionist; I do think that coordination makes a difference
and is necessary at the present time. The United States seem to be in
recovery, although Mundell has raised some doubts, which I share,
about the sustainability of the recovery.

My doubts spring from several sources. I shall mention only one, and that has to do with exchange rates. Let's suppose for the sake of argument a sluggish rest of the world—nothing happening basically, neither a deterioration nor a recovery. Under that assumption, the U.S. current-account deficit is going to become huge. At some point, the market is going to notice that and begin to worry about its sustainability. There could be a very sharp drop in the dollar exchange rate, à la 1978. This would be stimulative to the U.S. economy and depressive to the rest of the world, but those effects in the short run might be overwhelmed by the resulting turbulence in currency and financial markets generally. That could well set back the U.S. recovery. The United States is still the largest single national economy in the world, but it's a much smaller proportion of the world economy than it used to be, and while recovery in the United States tends to pull the rest of the world with it, it pulls with a very weak pull. And it pulls mainly through a weakening of the U.S. current account, which has possible costs both on the exchange-rate front and on the commercial front, where increased pressure for protection is all but inevitable. To avoid these costs, I think that some help is desirable for dealing with the external debt situation, both in the form of world recovery as a necessary condition and in the form of assistance from the other leading industrial countries; I am thinking of the same ones that Dr. Emminger mentioned this morning—Germany, Japan, and Britain.

The prescription that I would propose is that the United States should ease further on monetary policy. I would combine that with some fiscal restraint, but not to take effect at once. The Japanese, the Germans, and the British, if I understand the situation correctly, have had fiscal contraction in the autonomous sense—not in the observed deficits but in what Dr. Emminger calls the structural part of the deficit, which has been contracting. From a short-run or medium-run point of view, this is absolutely the wrong way to move. Such fiscal contraction should be postponed. The change in the policy mix would help world recovery, and would gradually ease the dollar down rather than risking the precipitous drop which I think might otherwise occur.

The reason for doing all this in a coordinated way is the one that I suggested in putting the question to Max Corden earlier—that the short-run trade-offs, as they appear to any single government acting alone, are worse than if what's done is part of a joint package. I focused on four countries; there are some smaller countries that also could join the bandwagon. I put this forward now really to provoke you; I want to know what's wrong with that set of proposals, and I have no doubt that tomorrow morning I'll get some answers.

*Hinshaw*: May I ask a question? I would hope that at some time during this conference we will consider the sort of questions that Robert Mundell and Robert Triffin have raised with regard to longer-run solutions to our problems in the international monetary area. Am I right in assuming that this is what's on the calendar tomorrow afternoon?

*Cooper*: What I would propose to do is to spend the morning on current macroeconomic issues and the afternoon on the nature of the system—that is, on what various people see as flaws or weaknesses or imperfections in the basic institutional arrangements—the kind of questions that Bob Mundell raised.

Roland Vaubel and
Members of the
Conference

# International Economic Coordination: The Way Out?

*Chairman Cooper*: I suggested last evening that we devote this morning's session to the current situation—that is to say, with a relatively short time horizon of, say, two to three years. This afternoon we can devote to the longer-term issues concerning the nature of the system and how the system perhaps should be changed. I tried in just a few minutes at the end of the last session to suggest an outline of a recovery program—just sketching it without going into the rationale— and I now open the floor to discussion of the recovery problem. I shall call first on Roland Vaubel.

*Vaubel*: I should like to ask a few heretical questions about the welfare-theory foundations of the case for international coordination of monetary and fiscal policies. I would be very grateful if you would allow about ten minutes for my statement, even if you disagree with me—which I'm afraid you will.

The first task is to define what we mean by international coordination. There are two meanings, both of which have been employed in our discussion. The first is that we simply have exchange of information between policy makers and that we make sure that everybody acts independently in the light of the full information that exists about the policy intentions of other policy makers. International coordination in that sense, I believe, is totally uncontroversial; it is desirable. But this does not mean that there have to be summit meetings to exchange the information, because that information would be useful not only for policy makers but for everybody. The second meaning of international coordination would be that policy makers sit together and negotiate about how they are going to use their policy instruments and even about what targets they are going to aim at. I believe that this type of coordination is controversial.

Now what arguments are advanced in favor of coordination in this second sense? Some are derived from assignment theory, some are derived from externality theory, and some are derived from game theory. If you will permit me, I shall go through them.

First, assignment theory. It is surprising that assignment theory is adduced in this case, because what assignment theory essentially tells us is that if we assign instruments to targets according to the comparative advantage of the instrument—that is, if, in Mundell's words, we have an effective market classification—then we can rely on decentralized decision-making; decentralized decision-making in government policy would be as efficient as decentralized decision-making in the market.

But this is what I believe Max Corden has called the naïve view, so let's become more sophisticated. The first apparent sophistication is the view that there may be inconsistencies in the targets among different nations—say, in exchange rates. Since the exchange rate is common to all, somehow consistency has to be achieved. We could say the same for the real interest rate, which essentially has to be equalized all over the world, and we could say the same for current-account positions, which mirror one another for different countries. But the inconsistency problem arises only if we regard the targets of policy makers as unconditionally fixed—that is, if we do not incorporate a target-adjusting mechanism. Jürg Niehans, in a paper which was published in the late 1960s, showed that there is such a target-adjusting mechanism. For example, a central bank, faced by the choice between an exchange-rate target and a price-level target, will not unconditionally adhere to the exchange-rate target; the action will depend on the price that has to be paid in terms of inflation or deflation. So, in fact, what we have are indifference curves for the policy makers. And since there is a target-adjusting mechanism both in the market and in the making of government policy, the inconsistency problem solves itself.

Now there are some—and this is the second assignment-theory argument—who say, "Okay, we can leave everything to decentralization, and a consistent constellation of targets will be achieved. But that may take a long time—too long a time—and therefore we need coordination." This, however, in my view, is simply an argument in favor of exchange of information, because if we exchange information about what we are going to do—and, in fact, about what we are going to do in alternative circumstances—then we can depict our reaction curves to others, and we can achieve the equilibrium position very promptly.

The third assignment-theory argument is that in some cases there may be a need for cross-assignment; that is, a policy instrument used in one country may have to be assigned to a target of another country. This I find hard to imagine. I think it is very difficult to

imagine that, say, German monetary policy should have a comparative advantage—as compared with U.S. monetary policy—in achieving price-level stability in the United States. But even if such cases
exist, all this means is that there has to be a once-and-for-all agreement on the efficient assignment of instruments to targets. Once that
has been achieved, no further coordination is needed; we have an effective target classification, and that's that.

Now let's consider externality-theory arguments. Whenever we
use externality theory, we have to be extremely careful to distinguish
between technological and pecuniary externalities—that is, between
externalities which are Pareto-relevant and those which are not. I
think there is general agreement that pecuniary externalities—those
externalities which arise merely from market interdependence—are
not Pareto-relevant; we don't have to worry about them. In fact, since
it is market interdependence which brings about a Pareto optimum,
these externalities are to be desired.

Now what are we dealing with here? We are dealing with international market interdependence. The decisions of a producer of
money in one country affect, through the market mechanism, the decisions of private agents in other countries. It's a bit like, say, Volks-
wagen making a path-breaking innovation which affects buyers and
sellers in all countries of the world—producers of cars and buyers
of cars. We would not want, for that reason, to have coordination or
collusion between car producers or between car producers and car
buyers.

There are some who believe that this argument applies only in a
"flexprice" world. I don't think that is correct. Even if we have prices
and wages adjusting with a lag, the argument applies, because the lag
can be due to two causes. For example, prices and wages may adjust
with a lag because there is a high economic cost to more rapid adjustment. In that case, the market is acting efficiently, and the costs
which arise are inevitable. The other possibility is that these costs
and these lags in adjustment are not inevitable and that they could be
avoided by government. I would suggest that if governments can do
something about it, they should use competition policy in order to
achieve a more rapid adjustment.

What I've said about externalities in the case of monetary and
fiscal policy does not apply to those policy actions which interfere
with the market mechanism, like protectionism. I believe that a
strong externality-theory case can be made for international negotiations relating to tariffs as well as to international public goods—for
example, to defense or to the law of the sea. These are perfectly legit-

imate issues for a summit meeting, but I'm afraid that the attention
to monetary and fiscal policy will divert attention from these other
issues that should be discussed at such a meeting. But even in the
field of monetary and fiscal policy, there is a public good involved,
and that is the public good of knowledge about proper monetary and
fiscal policies. If, let's say, one country adopts a more successful policy, and achieves a disinflation in that way, it provides knowledge to
other countries—to the voters in other countries—about the cause of
the inflation they are suffering from and about the remedies for that
suffering.

This is essentially what Hayek means by competition as a mechanism of discovery. If we have a diversity of efforts, those who are
more successful provide an example to those who are less successful,
and the less successful can take advantage of this. Incidentally,
knowledge is also provided in the form of predictability. If different
countries adopt different policies, then the world business cycle as a
whole will be dampened, and the increased stability will make prediction less difficult.

Now I come to my last point—on game theory. The argument
here is that we cannot look at the different countries as competitors.
There are too few of them; some are just too large, and thus have too
large an influence. So we have to use game theory. But I wonder
whether game theory provides the correct paradigm for this problem,
because it would assume that we are simply dealing with politicians
who are doing all they can for the welfare of their people. Of course,
we could use the alternative paradigm of self-interested politicians
colluding against the public. If we want to be cynical, we could para-
phrase Adam Smith and say that politicians seldom meet together
without the conversation ending in a contrivance to raise the money
supply and the price level. If, on the other hand, we have competition
between monetary-policy makers, then each monetary-policy maker
will be constrained by what other monetary-policy makers do, because if one country inflates more than the others, there will be an
exit from its currency, there will be a decline in the exchange rate,
and very soon the country will be forced to reverse its inflationary
policies. That is exactly what appears to have happened in 1977–78
in the United States. So, having examined the various arguments, I
wonder whether there is a serious, sound, welfare-theory basis for the
international coordination of monetary and fiscal policies.

*Cooper*: Does anyone here want to speak directly to this very interesting exposition, which—apart from the case of genuine international public goods—is, as I interpret it, an argument against not

only summit meetings but against any meetings of ministers for purposes other than the exchange of information? Also—Vaubel can correct me if I'm wrong—apart from areas where there are public goods or genuine nonpecuniary external economies, it's an argument against any country complaining about the policies of any other country. Nicky Kaldor wants to comment.

*Kaldor*: I just want to ask one simple question. Vaubel mentioned a situation of imperfect competition where there is a limited number of firms, each facing a downward-sloping demand curve—a situation in which there is both excess capacity and unemployment. So production could be expanded, but no single producer finds it profitable to expand production; that is to say, optimizing profits wouldn't allow the producers to increase output. Now suppose that all the various producers get together and coordinate their actions, each of them agreeing to increase production by $X$ percent. Since the market for any one producer depends on the incomes earned by all the other firms, coordination would make it possible to expand the production of all, because, under that condition, the demand would expand *pari passu* with the increase in supply. Now what's wrong with this case?

*Vaubel*: How do you apply the case? Who are the firms—the policy makers or the market?

*Kaldor*: Well, I don't know what you mean by policy makers and the market. Each firm decides for itself what output and at what price to sell, and knows that it has a limited market; it can only sell a limited amount at a given price. It could sell a little more if it lowered the price, but that would not be profitable; profits would fall if the demand curve is given. But if all producers expand production, then the demand curve for each firm will shift at the same time that output shifts, and the firms will all find that they can produce more, employ more people, and use their capacity more fully. Everyone is better off.

*Vaubel*: I understand what you are saying, but the question is how we apply that to the problem at hand. There are two possibilities: Either the firms you are mentioning should be equated with the policy makers who coordinate or the firms should be equated with the economy which the policy makers face. If the second is the case, then I wonder why you do not recommend such coordination between all producers, say, of cars in Britain.

*Kaldor*: I'm sorry; I did not mean to imply that there is only one industry. The agreement would have to cover all firms in the same position. I don't distinguish between $X$ industry and $Y$ industry.

*Jamison*: I'd like to say that, in our country [the United States], you'd have some problems with antitrust laws, for sure.

*Cooper*: Yes, but Nicky is addressing the conceptual problem. Maybe I can rephrase the question. Vaubel put his observations in the context of policy coordination, but if I understood his arguments correctly, what they boil down to, with the exceptions that he noted, is a case for decentralized, as opposed to centralized, decision-making. The fact that he is talking about policy makers is secondary. Nicky's example happens to involve firms, but he's suggesting that centralized or coordinated decision-making results in a superior outcome to decentralized decision-making. James Meade has a two-handed intervention.

*Meade*: May I interpret Nicky's intervention in a way which, I think, is directly relevant to Vaubel's masterly exposition? In Nicky's exposition, let each firm be a country. In the British case, the persons in charge of this firm are the governor of the Bank of England and the chancellor of the Exchequer. Now if these two gentlemen say, "We will expand this economy," the terms of trade will turn against it, because I'm assuming that the United Kingdom is still big enough to affect the terms of trade. And if country B is the United States, and the United States expands, the terms of trade will turn against that country. But if both countries get together and say, "We will both expand at the same time," Nicky's parable is absolutely relevant here; the foreign demand for each country's exports will expand, and the expansion will take place without any adverse movement in the terms of trade for either country. Now both countries, perhaps rightly or perhaps wrongly, may have thought that the game wasn't worth the candle if they had to face a deterioration in the terms of trade. But it is worth the candle if they don't. Isn't that a fair analogy?

*Cooper*: And, at a formal level, the same analogy applies to tariff negotiations. One of the inhibitions to unilateral tariff reductions is the possible deterioration in the terms of trade, but reciprocal tariff reductions don't have this result.

*Meade*: Exactly.

*Gutowski*: I doubt that Lord Kaldor's example is correct. Under imperfect competition, you *always* have underutilization of capacity in a certain sense. If there is reason for a firm to expand, it means that the firm is not at the maximum-profit position. If it is not, there is reason for other firms to enter the market. That is the normal model of imperfect competition.

*Kaldor*: That interpretation is incorrect; it has been blown up by myself, by Machlup, and by a lot of other people. I don't want to go into it, but if you want me to, I can explain it in two minutes.

*Gutowski*: But let me go one step further. If all firms expand together, that would mean—if they are in equilibrium at the outset—that the losses for the firms would be small for each, but they would be losses. If only one firm were to expand, it would have a bigger loss than if all were to expand. But what is the mechanism which, if all firms expand together, would lead to a position where they not only cover costs, as they did before, but where they even make profits—which you would have to assume in order to make the example relevant?

*Kaldor*: Well, each firm's expansion creates additional incomes. Of course, only a very small part of the output of a firm is sold to the people working for that firm. You may manufacture nails, but the people whom you employ spend only a small proportion of their income on nails. So employing more people doesn't increase the demand for your product by more than a small fraction of your additional outlay. But if all firms do that, then the additional demand may well correspond to the additional outlay, because the employees as a group spend their incomes on the products of their own firms plus the products of all the other firms.

*Hinshaw*: My comment is purely procedural. Our words here are being recorded on tape with the intention of immortalizing them in a book, and it is therefore very important that we all talk directly into our microphones. I should add that everything that's said here is on the record unless the speaker explicitly indicates that a particular remark is off the record.

*Corden*: My remark is absolutely on the record. I was going to intervene right after Lord Kaldor's statement to say that I agree with him; I'm trying to get three points of agreement during this conference. He and I are now agreed on two points, and let me give an example to support the second point. It is exactly the same example that James Meade has just given—namely, that expansion by one country would worsen its terms of trade, especially in a two-country model, and that, to maintain employment, there would have to be a fall in real wages in the expanding country, whereas if both countries expand, they can avoid this situation.

*Kaldor*: I agree with what you said—except that, to be more realistic, I would not talk about changes in the terms of trade, but of imbalances in the current account. Let us suppose that the world consists of two countries; call them Germany and France. Suppose, to start out, that the balance of payments between the two countries is in equilibrium; in terms of value, Germany exports as much to France as France exports to Germany. But let us assume that both countries are in an underemployment equilibrium; both have unemployed workers and equipment, and both could produce more.

Now let us suppose that, in France, a new expansionist government comes into power, and decides to introduce stimulus into the budget. In Germany, things remain the same. Well, the result of that is that France buys more from Germany without Germany buying more from France, so France is faced with a balance-of-payments crisis. But if, before introducing this expansionary budget, Mr. Mitterand were to go to Bonn and convince the German chancellor, whoever he was, that he should simultaneously put into effect the same expansionist policies, then it is perfectly possible that, as a result of the German expansion, the German demand for French goods would increase as much as the French demand for German goods. Both countries would be better off as a result of coordinated policies of expansion. And you don't need to invoke price elasticities—only income elasticities. The prices might remain the same.

*Corden*: All of our discussion this morning about coordinated international expansion relates in one way or another to general-equilibrium theory, and I would like to say a few words about that. The crucial issue, it seems to me, is whether the expansion is a small divisible expansion—a marginal increase—or is one that involves indivisibilities. If you have to make large-scale indivisible decisions, then you are dependent on the expansion of other firms—or other countries—and thus, in the case of countries, there is a strong case for international coordination. But if you are making decisions involving small divisible movements, as is customarily assumed in general-equilibrium theory, then coordination is not called for. I think that's the underlying analytical issue here.

Let me add another comment. I have great sympathy for the approach that Professor Vaubel has put forward, not just in dealing with the question of optimality of the world system, but in trying to understand how the system is operating at this very moment. After all, we have to face reality; none of the plans that various people in this room and others have devised have been accepted, yet the system is in some sense equilibrating. Thus we need to ask ourselves: What are the laws behind this system that is now operating? And the way I look at it is that we have a market system in which governments are participants along with private firms. Governments borrow and lend on the world capital market, and intervene—that is, buy and sell—in the foreign-exchange market. They all have implicit utility functions, just as firms have profit-maximizing functions, and the system equilibrates, in practice, through a world market. So there is an underlying market structure behind the present system.

Now Professor Vaubel has gone further. I've been talking just about the existence of equilibrium, not about its optimality. Vaubel is arguing that, subject to all the textbook qualifications, the world system, with governments included as participants, is in some sense optimal for the world, on the assumption that each government knows what is best for its own people—just as we assume that each firm knows what's best for the firm. But the difficulty, when we talk about economic efficiency or about optimality in the Paretian sense, is that we are brushing aside the distribution issue—the income-division issue. So we can't really say that the system is optimal; we can only say that it's efficient. Of course, governments may pursue independent internal policies of redistribution, in which case all the issues arise that Lord Kaldor and others have written about. But there is no such systematic redistribution going on between countries, so that, even though all the decentralized decisions may be Pareto-efficient for the world as a whole, they will not necessarily lead to the most desirable outcome for each particular country. And that, of course, leads to pressures between countries. I can't go deeper into this, but I thought it might be useful to raise these issues.

*Cooper*: Bob, do you want to comment on this before we go on?

*Mundell*: Yes; the analogy between the firm and the country, I think, has to be qualified by the fact that if all firms expand, then, with a downward-sloping demand curve for the industry, all firms may suffer losses. So we have to start out by assuming some kind of disequilibrium or distortion, such as a situation of unemployment and excess capacity, as Armin Gutowski mentioned.

Much of what has been said here relates to Say's Law: Supply creates its own demand. Now there's a lot of truth to Say's Law. It isn't true, of course, that there can never be an overall glut of something in the short run. There can be mass unemployment as we have experienced, so the law can't be completely true. But the law is true in the sense that if, under conditions of unemployment and excess capacity, all firms expand, then income, expenditure, and employment will also expand. So I think that the need for coordination may arise when we have a basic distortion.

In a state of depression, it is also important for there to be incentives for expansion. This is where tax cuts come into the picture. In a profit system, tax cuts make it possible for firms to expand. The tax cuts can go in two directions; they can go to consumers, who then will buy more, or they can go to firms, which will be induced to invest in additional plant and equipment. Or, better still, they can go to both consumers and business. This approach, I might say, is very different from increased government spending, which, contrary to the usual Keynesian model, has a much smaller impact on the stimulation of demand because of the financing requirements on the part of government.

*Heller*: I think it's important to ask ourselves why we are where we are, economically speaking, and also to ask ourselves just how and where we are going to expand. First, why are we where we are? Why are we suddenly in a position of 10 percent unemployment and 25 percent underutilization of capacity? It's not because people just didn't want all these goods in the first place. And firms didn't voluntarily invest in the excess capacity because they wanted to have excess capacity around. In most cases, I think, it has been a matter of a change in relative prices that has brought about such a situation, and we can easily identify instances in the present world where that has happened. We have sectoral imbalances, so the generalized theory of overall excess capacity—let's expand everything at the same time— really doesn't apply. If the problem were a simple one, we could just legislate a wage increase—give everybody a 10 percent higher wage— but that would obviously be self-defeating. In any case, I don't think we are in a situation where all we have to do is to stimulate aggregate demand.

*Kaldor*: The question is what we should do if we *were* in a situation of overall excess capacity, and that question you haven't answered.

*Hinshaw*: This is simply a modest point about price effects. Lord Kaldor said earlier that a generalized increase in demand might not have any effect on prices. One can imagine several different situations. Certainly, in a classical constant-cost world—if one can assume unemployment of workers and equipment in such a world—an increase in demand would not have any price effects. Similarly, in a Keynesian underemployment equilibrium, with mass unemployment and general excess capacity, there could be a considerable expansion of demand without much effect on prices. Indeed, in a world of imperfect competition and of general excess capacity, the initial effect on prices of an overall increase in demand might conceivably, as Roy Harrod used to argue, be downward. I think this is an important question that needs to be thought through.

*Cooper*: If I may step out of the chair for a moment, I think Mr. Vaubel has given us an extremely useful taxonomy of arguments that might be advanced for international coordination of policy. I have tried to think of cases where there have been systematic attempts to coordinate policy—four come to mind—and then have tried to fit them into his categories. One which he himself mentioned is tariff negotiations. Here, for historical reasons, we inherit a level of protection which we're unhappy with collectively, but, for various reasons, unilateral tariff reduction is not easy or is impossible to undertake. A second is the area of East-West trade. We have big disagreements in that area, but the disagreements are not over the need for coordination but over what the content of the coordination should be.

A third area where there have been systematic attempts in recent years toward coordination is energy policy. I would suggest that this falls into Vaubel's category of pecuniary externalities—not nonpecuniary externalities—but nonetheless I would say that the coordination was entirely appropriate, even if not completely successful. This was a case—I have in mind 1974 and, even more, 1979–80—where, to put the matter somewhat loosely, panic in the world oil market was driving oil prices way up and where, I think, every country had some incentive, by virtue of the rising prices, to conserve energy. But the collective incentive of all of them was greater than the sum of the individual incentives of each of them, precisely because of the influence on the terms of trade. If each of them (I have in mind the major industrial consumers) could act together, then they had some reasonable hope of influencing the terms of trade—in this case, the rate of increase of oil prices—whereas each country alone would consider itself as negligible, or next to negligible, in the world market, and therefore would have little incentive to act unilaterally. This is a pecuniary externality, but it's one which falls into the Mundell category, since it originates from an imperfection—namely, the oligopolistic structure of the other side of the market. And if there are oligopolistic producers, then it may make some sense to have an oligopoly among consumers in order to take effective counteraction.

The fourth area is macroeconomics—really the implicit topic of this morning's conversation. And there I'd like to make one point about Vaubel's acceptance of full exchange of information. He said it just in passing, but I want to underline it. Full information in this context—I think he would agree—does not just mean exchange of factual information, but exchange of information on contingent reactions by each party. It's an extremely complex exchange of information that must take place to meet this criterion: If you do the following, I will do the following; if you do something else, I will do something else, and so forth. Moreover, as Max Corden reminded us, we don't go to parliaments with requests for infinitesimally small changes in taxes or expenditures; we can't go that often. Some countries only go once a year; others can go more frequently, but with great reluctance, for a supplemental budget of some kind—at most, twice a year, but any change is always discrete, not infinitesimal.

I would suggest that in these circumstances the difference between full exchange of information, including contingent reactions by each party, and a negotiation over what each party will do, in practice disappears. The fellows sitting around the table exchanging their information on their contingent reaction functions are, in effect, negotiating. And I'm not sure, therefore, whether the distinction in practice is worth making. Of course, if the parties don't exchange full information on contingent reaction functions, there can be very long lags which are Pareto-suboptimal from the point of view of each and every country taken separately. In fact, there can even be dynamic instability. Max talked about optimality; he didn't talk about instability, but it is possible, if there are sequential actions which are reactive in nature, to have an unstable system. I think, therefore, that just saying "full exchange of information" buries a lot. The result in practice is a negotiation which, incidentally, cannot be undertaken by officials; it has to be undertaken by political leaders, because officials don't know the reaction functions of their political leaders.

*Mundell*: It has to be undertaken by dictators, in fact.

*Cooper*: If one understands political leaders to be those who put propositions to their parliaments, they don't have to be dictators. It's understood in modern democracies that no prime minister or chancellor or president can be sure of delivering on a policy; all he can do is promise to work for it. Well, I think we ought to give Mr. Vaubel a chance to respond.

*Vaubel*: My main point on this is that it's not a case for anything clandestine; full information is useful for everybody, and therefore this information should be exchanged in public. But my more fundamental point is that all those here who have objected to my conclusions have rejected the competitive framework as applicable to the problem at hand.

*Kaldor*: Have rejected the *perfectly* competitive framework; that distinction is very important.

*Vaubel*: But that means that my objections to the game-theory argument still apply. My main argument against the game-theory case for international coordination is that it assumes that politicians not only know what is best, but actually do what is best, for their countries. I see a very fundamental difference between the interests of politicians and the interests of the people.

*Kaldor*: Everybody knows that.

*Vaubel*: Okay; if that's the case, then it's in the interest of the people to have competition between the politicians—as much competition as possible. Now the main argument that came up for international coordination was the terms-of-trade argument. That argument can be seen in a rather different perspective. What we are talking about is that if one country, individually, expands the money supply, then the exchange rate will immediately depreciate, and therefore the inflation which results from the increase in the money supply will come faster than if all countries do the same thing. So the question is whether it is desirable to lengthen the lag with which the price level will react to the money-supply increase. The politicians, of course, have an interest in lengthening the lag—especially before an election. My argument is that it is undesirable to lengthen the lag; it is much better to see the consequences immediately so that people will know who is responsible for what.

*Kaldor*: Do you mean that if you increase the volume of credit generated by the banks in order to enable firms to increase production, this is inflationary, and results in an increase in the price level? Is that what you're saying?

*Vaubel*: I'm saying that the money supply affects the price level regardless of whether you have unemployment or not.

*Kaldor*: Well, you're wrong.

*Cooper*: If I may say so, I think there's a critical difference in judgment here over the way economies work. In Nicky's model of the world, with unemployment of resources, an increase in the money supply will be inflationary if a single country acts alone under floating exchange rates, but that if countries expand together, you won't get this increase in the price level.

*Vaubel*: Well, in Nicky's view of the world, there shouldn't be stagflation, should there?

*Kaldor*: Why shouldn't there be? But if all firms agree that they are going to expand output by 10 percent, they will need extra credit from their banks.

*Heller*: But we should be clear that the initial situation of unemployment was not the result of malice; firms didn't get together and say, "We'll cut output by 10 percent and create some unemployment."

*Kaldor*: My basic point is that under imperfect competition there is absolutely no reason to suppose that we are in a full-employment, maximum-output situation.

*Corden*: I think we are mixing up two separate issues that could really be disentangled. One issue is whether we believe that there is a possibility of short-run unemployment of an involuntary nature.

*Kaldor*: Or long-run unemployment.

*Corden*: Well, for the moment, let's take just the short run. For example, I would take the view that it's possible to have short-run Keynesian-style unemployment—that is, a nonvertical short-run Phillips Curve—whereas, I think, implicit in Vaubel's view is really the rational-expectations type of model.

*Cooper*: That's right.

*Corden*: In other words, a vertical Phillips Curve. Now that's one issue that's been under the surface here, but I think we should keep this separate from what seem to be the more interesting issues—very important issues—that Vaubel has raised about the system's operation. I think we could concede the possibility of Keynesian unemployment, and could have different views as to whether it's short-run or long-run, but could still regard Vaubel's framework as highly useful. We could take the view that politicians are not the horrible people that he is implying, but that they are responsible, well-meaning, kindly people—people like Keynes and Professor Meade—

*Meade* [*smiling*]: Yes, yes.

*Corden*: People that are looking after the interests of their own countries. Let's assume that each of them is making his own judgment as to what Keynesian or non-Keynesian policies are appropriate and that the decision-making process is decentralized. We can still argue that there is a system for the world as a whole which (A) tends to an equilibrium of some kind and (B) tends to some kind of efficiency, subject to qualifications. I don't think Vaubel is saying that the system, a priori, is necessarily efficient. But we do have the competitive model as a reference point, and can then go through all the reasons why there may be inefficiencies and a need for intervention. Similarly, in thinking about the question of coordination, we first have a simple model which implies—given ten or fifteen assumptions—that there is no need for coordination; decentralized governmental and private decision-making is sufficient. But then we think the matter through, step by step, looking for reasons for intervention or coordination or planning, and so on. The model gives us an analytical framework for thinking rigorously about this whole issue, but we should regard it as a starting point rather than as an end.

*Mundell*: I think it's a starting point, but a marvelous one. The point I want to raise is the tremendous power of this exchange of information, especially if we know the contingent reaction functions. If we had such a system in the political world, we would never have any wars. Certainly, the Argentine-British war would never have taken place if everybody knew what the British would do and what the Argentines would do. We wouldn't have had a Second World War or a First World War. We wouldn't have any strikes.

*Kaldor*: There would be no need for peace treaties.

*Mundell*: And we'd never have tariffs except in those curious cases where a country gains by a tariff regardless of what other countries do. In fact, if we had complete exchange of information of this type, we would never be in a suboptimal position. And in that case we would never have need for any kind of alteration of policy. But the question in the economic world, and of course in the political world, is: How do we get that complete exchange of information?

*Cooper*: And the answer is that we cannot, because politicians and countries don't know their complete contingent reaction functions. They operate in a great mist, in which a few things show dimly, and it's only as they move forward into the mist and see some shapes take a little form that they decide what they're going to do next. That's the trouble with that.

*Mundell*: But there's a further political implication. If we follow this up without our moral hats on, wouldn't we end up by doing what 80 percent of the world has done—move toward dictatorship?

*Cooper*: But dictators don't have any clearer idea than democratic leaders do about what their contingent reaction functions are. That's my observation, anyway.

*Mundell*: You may be right, but that's not the end of the chess game. The next move is from many dictators to one dictator; we have one global dictator, and he always knows what he's going to do. And if we have a one-world system with a single dictator, then there's no need for exchange of information except inside the head of the dictator.

*Gutowski*: Perhaps we needn't go that far; we could have just one president for a world central bank!

I think, Mr. Chairman, that you made the decisive remark; the dissent is over the question of how economic systems work—not economies in general, but particular economies. Individual economies work differently, and that is the major point. It's not just the reaction functions of politicians—those you can possibly change—but the effects of particular policy instruments are different in different countries. And so are the opinions about those effects. For example, at the Bonn summit, we in Germany agreed to increase demand by 1 percent of GNP. In our view, this was a sacrifice. But it was looked at

quite differently in other countries, which felt that our economy
would work in such a way that the 1 percent increase would help us.
We felt that it was a sacrifice, though it might help other countries.
Some Germans felt that it would not even help other countries, because they had quite a different perspective from that of foreign economists about how economic systems work.

So this is a real problem, and I don't think it is really a question
of exchange of information. It's not that simple. And we're not talking about a zero-sum game. In war, there is the same question. Wars
are started because people have different perceptions of how the war
would work—of what the outcome would be. There is the old joke
that Hitler would never start a war; he had only to look at the map,
which would show Germany to be very small and the United States
very big. And the punch line was, "But does he know it?" Well, of
course he knew how small Germany was and how big the other
countries were, but he had the perception that Germany would fight
in a completely different way and thus would be able to win. He assumed that other countries would react to his actions with bombs
and whatnot, but he didn't expect to lose. I don't think we should go
too far with this analogy, because we are not talking about a situation in which one country would lose what another country gains;
we have the overall perception that all could gain, but we have different perceptions about how this could be achieved.

*Meade*: I would like first of all to say how much I have appreciated and, indeed, have learned from Roland Vaubel's exposition,
which I think is an extremely good way of thinking of the problem of
coordination. But there is one question—I hate to repeat it, but I
didn't understand his answer—which is relevant to what we're talking about now. I understood Mr. Vaubel to say that tariff negotiations
were a legitimate form of externality public good. I cannot understand why the same argument doesn't apply to mutual expansion and
the terms of trade.

Let me put this possible problem to Mr. Vaubel and ask him to
tell me where I'm wrong. I'm going to assume that politicians are
good men like Maynard Keynes in trying to put the world right. Now
Vaubel may say that it all depends on that, and if it all depends on
that, I will just shut up. If it doesn't all depend on that, suppose there
are two countries, both of which have lots of unemployed resources
and lots of needs that could be fulfilled. And suppose we could devise
measures to expand demand and output (I'm not going to say what
these measures are; that would immediately invite a quarrel between
monetarists and Keynesians). Perhaps Vaubel will say, "That's not

possible," but suppose it were possible; there are good men, and they could do that inside each country. If one country expands, and the other does not, the expanding country will lose on the terms of trade; if both countries expand, there will be no such loss for either country (don't ask me what model I have in mind; I'm sure there are models that will lend to that). Now why isn't the argument for coordinated expansion in these conditions the same as the argument for reciprocal tariff reductions? That's my basic problem, and it is basic, I think, to the application of Mr. Vaubel's excellent analysis.

*Vaubel*: Very briefly, the difference between the tariff case and the monetary-policy case is that, in tariff negotiations, you are dealing with a policy instrument which interferes with the market process, and therefore involves technological externalities, whereas, in money-supply negotiations, you are dealing with a policy instrument which works entirely through the market, and therefore involves only pecuniary externalities. Now the question, as you said, is about assumptions. I would disagree with your assumptions, and would say that there is no policy instrument with which you can increase real demand in such a way that it would be worth the cost of doing so.

*Meade*: I don't want to get into details, but Vaubel did say monetary policy. I wouldn't do it by monetary policy; I'd do it by fiscal policy. But in a sense, yes, it is pecuniary. It is not a technological externality if the terms of trade move; it simply means that, by expanding in one country, we're making people better off, but some of the people we're making better off are the people in the other country. That's a distributive effect, but it doesn't demolish the case for coordination.

*Gutowski*: Professor Meade, I'm wondering about your assumptions. Take the case of Germany. Let us say that we Germans feel that by reducing the fiscal deficit we could have lower interest rates and, from the resulting increase in private investment, could increase our GNP by $X$ percent. Another country might say, "We will increase demand by fiscal expansion, and this will increase our GNP $X$ percent." Thus there won't be any detrimental effect on the terms of trade. But the real dispute would be that our country would say, "If you increase the fiscal deficit, you will have inflation," and the other country would say, "Your policy will reduce GNP, not increase it." I think that is the issue.

*Cooper*: But we're trying to sort the two things out. There is unquestionably dispute over how economies actually work, and I suspect, as you do, that this is the central issue—not whether or not there should be coordination. But Vaubel has raised a different issue—namely, whether coordination is worthwhile. In response to questions, his position on coordination is always negative, which is somewhat troubling.

*Gutowski*: But is there a need for coordination if the national policies work? In that case, the countries would pursue them anyway.

*Cooper*: No; the necessity for coordination arises because the trade-offs to a country are very different if it acts alone than if it acts on the clear understanding that the other countries are going to act too. The opportunity set that the decision-makers face is actually different in the two situations.

*Meade*: That's what I'm saying.

*Cooper*: What is needed is not just an exchange of factual information but full sets of contingency reactions.

*Gutowski*: Right.

*Cooper*: Information which the authorities themselves typically do not have.

*Corden*: Let me add to the clarification or confusion, whichever it is. Mr. Vaubel is saying that an expansion of the money supply will not raise real output at home and therefore will not worsen the country's terms of trade. Professor Meade is saying that an expansion of aggregate nominal demand may, at least, raise real output at home, which is good for the home country, and, in addition, is likely to worsen the country's terms of trade, thus improving the opportunity set for the foreign country. Given this assumption and given that the foreign country is in the same situation, one can make a case for policy coordination through the terms of trade. But of course if one doesn't subscribe to the basic assumption that an expansion of nominal demand will have an effect on real output or on the terms of trade, then the subject is closed.

*Cooper*: Exactly.

*Corden*: Then an additional quite separate issue is the one raised by Professor Gutowski, which is a difference of opinion between the two countries as to whether a fiscal expansion is desirable from the point of view of the inflation-unemployment trade-off.

*Mundell*: The answer to Professor Meade's provocative question was provided in the literature thirty-three years ago.

*Meade*: I don't read; I write.

*Mundell*: Well, the book was written by you. In the mathematical supplement to your treatise on the balance of payments, you gave a very explicit analysis of these matters. In a two-country model, you showed the effect on the terms of trade of tariff changes and of

changes in output when undertaken unilaterally and when undertaken by both countries. Except in one case, you showed that, where
there is unemployment and excess capacity, a country, even when
acting unilaterally, will always gain from economic expansion, because the growth in output will exceed the income lost from the deterioration in the terms of trade. In that situation, theoretically, you
don't need international coordination, because there will be a gain for
both countries, though the other country perhaps gains more than its
share.

*Cooper*: This has been a most stimulating discussion, but let me
get back to Vaubel. I'm going to cloud the issue even further by qual-
ifying the statement about full provision of information. Let's assume
that we have Meade-type policy makers, who are well-meaning and
effective trustees for their nations, so we avoid the problem of politicians having different objective functions than the public. Even under
this assumption, there are game-theory situations in which it is in
the interest of a country not to provide full information. The most
fascinating example we've seen recently is Saudi Arabia bargaining
with other members of OPEC over the distribution of the cuts in oil
production, which all OPEC countries thought to be necessary. In
such a situation, an enormous game of bluff and counter-bluff goes
on. And distributional considerations lead to game-theory situations
in which full information is not desirable from the point of view of
each of the participants, taken separately, and in which the only way
to get action at all is a collective one.

I shall now give the floor to Mr. Matthes, who has been very pa-
tient through all this discussion.

*Matthes*: I feel that my role here is to be more down-to-earth.

*Cooper*: On immediate issues?

*Matthes*: On issues of practical economic policy. You asked what
was wrong with your scenario of yesterday afternoon, in which you
suggested a new locomotive exercise on the part of Germany, Japan,
and Britain to counter the danger of a weakening of the U.S. dollar.
This weakening, you thought, would accompany the swing in the
U.S. current-account position.

Well, to my mind, there are at least two objections one could
raise. First, a deterioration in the U.S. current account by no means
automatically implies a weakening of the dollar, which is the preemi-
nent reserve currency of the Western world. As long as the deterioration of the current account is accompanied by a reasonable degree of
domestic price stability, the United States—because it provides a reserve currency—can experience such a deterioration without auto-

matic implications for the exchange rate. The previous experiences which contradict this were always ones in which the United States had a rising trend of inflation.

My second point concerns the likelihood of a successful outcome of a new locomotive exercise. In assessing this, I think one has to draw a balance sheet of the first exercise, which, to put it mildly, was not very successful. There were several reasons. Perhaps the most important was that the locomotive was set in motion when the German current account was already in a deteriorating condition. But this deterioration was visible only in volume terms, though at an early stage. For example, in a market-share analysis of the OECD type, it was clear that the German market share had gone down for years before the locomotive was set in motion. This situation was masked by the appreciation of the D-mark, and the only place—apart, of course, from the Bundesbank—where the true situation was more or less clearly seen was the IMF, which as early as 1977–78 recognized that the underlying German position had greatly deteriorated. That being so—and the situation being further aggravated by the second oil crisis—the immediate response to the sizable addition to German demand brought about by the Bonn summit was a drastic deterioration in the current account of the order of DM 50 billion. This brought Germany under external constraint, with important consequences for German interest-rate policy. In this connection, it should be noted that the D-mark has become the second most important reserve currency in the world and that it is therefore important that funds held in this form do not become volatile.

On balance, then, it seems very doubtful that the first locomotive exercise did any good for the rest of the world. I see no additional expansion; I see rather the reverse. And I conclude that our neighbors had to pay dearly for the expansionary stimulus they received in 1978 and 1979.

But what about the present situation? The German current account is certainly in a more viable position than in 1978–79, though by no means in chronic surplus. The other change, however, is that fiscal policy, as Dr. Emminger pointed out, now has much less room for maneuver than during the first locomotive exercise. The Christian Democrats based their whole election campaign on the scandalous state of German public finance and the scandal of the huge public debt. The public has become much more aware of the budget-deficit issue, and the expectation of a rising deficit would immediately lead to rising interest rates. So I conclude that it is very unlikely that, on balance, a new locomotive exercise would do any good for the world economy.

*Cooper*: I have a very different view of the history that you describe, but this is not the place to discuss it. I would like, though, to ask one question. You've suggested that German policy is now tightly constrained and that if it were to break out of this constraint in an economic expansion, the effect would be perverse. Does it follow from this that if there were a break out of that constraint in the opposite direction, the effect would be stimulative? That is to say, is it your view that a sharp contraction of the German budget deficit, say through an increase in taxes, would in fact have a stimulative effect on the German economy?

*Matthes*: Well, Mr. Chairman, I don't think there is an absolute symmetry in the situation. However, I wouldn't rule out the possibility; I would go as far as that.

*Cooper*: Well, there need not be symmetry, but it's a strong statement to say that an important government can have no influence on the course of macroeconomic events at home and abroad; that would make sense only under very special circumstances.

*Gutowski*: May I comment? The structural part of our deficit was reduced by much more than we ourselves expected. I think the reduction of the structural deficit was about DM 16 billion.

*Matthes*: Yes.

*Gutowski*: Instead of DM 9 billion, as was expected. But it can be argued that this had a positive effect on our economy, because it tended to reduce interest rates and to reduce inflation, thus assisting in the recent pickup in Germany.

*Cooper*: But this goes back to the distinction we were making earlier this morning between the desirability or not of coordinating, on the one hand, as against the particular actions to be taken as part of that coordination. And if there is a wide consensus on the functioning of the German economy in this regard—that Germany could contribute to expansion through, say, a tax increase—that doesn't preclude German participation in a coordinated action; it just means that the particular actions that the Germans take to achieve the common objective would be different ones. That's why I think this distinction we're making this morning is important.

*Corden*: I should like to focus on what I think is the central macroeconomic issue that is likely to arise in the years immediately ahead. It's highly likely that we'll get some kind of economic expansion. I don't know precisely when, nor do I know exactly how much of it will be the result of monetary policy relaxation; the techniques are subsidiary. But let's assume that it has happened. For a limited period, we'll be in this wonderful world, with a substantially higher level of employment and output, and with a lower level of inflation. Inflation, as we all know, has already gone down, and will probably stay down for a little while.

Now the central question is: Will we get another wage explosion? We ought now to think about it, because that is going to be the issue within, say, one or two years. If wages can't be restrained, we're just going to be back on the same treadmill.

In dealing with this problem, it seems to me that there are two separate issues. One of them is inflationary expectations. Assume for a moment that the unions want only to maintain real wages; then, of course, if they expect prices to rise, nominal wages will increase and create the usual problems. So the important thing here, I feel, is for governments to commit themselves that they will not ratify a new wage inflation. Now how they do this with conviction, given all the past history, I don't know, and perhaps we should give some thought here later to this particular problem.

But there's a second issue which I've also had some difficulty resolving. Nominal wages are likely to increase not only because of inflationary expectations and the desire just to maintain real wages, but also because there's likely to be an attitude that the world is back on course, that things are wonderful again, that prospects are great, and therefore that real wages can increase. So we may well get a rise in nominal wages with the intention of raising real wages. The more the feeling gets around that we're back in a boom, the more this will happen. We had this situation in Australia just a few years ago, when there was much talk about a forthcoming boom that never materialized. Immediately, wages increased with the intention of raising real wages, and the result was a major macroeconomic crisis. Now the moral I derive is that governments must somehow correct this idea; they must preach that things are not going to be really better and that there isn't going to be a great boom. Much better would be the state of mind in countries like Japan or Singapore, where people always feel that things are going to be bad; that's the attitude you want from the point of view of wage restraint.

Now the difficulty I have with this proposal—and therefore I am laying it on the table as a problem and not as a proposal—is that we also want to increase private investment to restore growth; we want to increase the inducement to invest. One way of doing it, of course, is to increase profitability. This is achieved to some extent by wage restraint. But another way of doing it is to raise animal spirits, to increase the optimism about the world.

*Kaldor*: To increase demand.

*Corden*: Okay, but let's assume that we have just increased demand. If we increase demand and at the same time tell everybody that there isn't going to be much growth and that things are going to be bad again, that may inhibit investment. From the point of view of fostering investment, we want to make people feel that we're back in a boom situation. But we don't want the unions to feel this. How we resolve that, I don't know, but I think it's a genuine issue in the years immediately ahead.

*Kaldor*: I don't disagree with anything you've said, but you left some important things unsaid. You talk about inflationary expectations, and you talk about a real recovery in terms of output and employment, yet you say nothing about commodity prices. The experience of the last ten years, even when nothing much was happening to the level of employment and output, has been that commodity prices are quite capable of rising by 50 percent or more in a few months. This creates a price inflation in itself, even before wages have had time to begin a rise. How are you going to deal with that situation? It ought not to be left out of account, because I think that, quantitatively, it is a bigger obstacle, even, than wages to any economic recovery that lasts more than a few months.

*Podbielski*: I can speak only for my own country, Italy, where the recession started much later, but if economic expansion gets under way again along the same pattern that we had before—without any structural changes in the pattern of investment or in wage arrangements—it will come to an end rather rapidly.

*Giuseppe Pennisi*: I would like to support the view just expressed by Dr. Podbielski. I'm also an Italian, but I lived in the United States for quite a number of years, and was able to observe American policies. Listening to the discussion this morning, I have the impression that we have been talking here about short-term solutions for what is basically a long-term structural problem.

*Cooper*: Are you speaking now of Italy or of the United States?

*Pennisi*: I am speaking of the OECD countries. I think we have to ask ourselves how we got into our present difficulties. There have been a number of reasons, of course—the wage-price spiral, inflationary expectations, and so on—but since the end of the 1960s the most important reason, I think, has been that we have been investing poorly.

*Kaldor*: We have been what?

*Pennisi*: Investing unwisely—both in the public and in the private sectors. The real rate of return, on public and private investments alike, has been low. That's the main reason why we got ourselves into this mess. We have been talking here about international coordination, but the basic problem of coordination is not concerned with essentially short-term strategies; the important question is how we can coordinate longer-term strategies. As an Italian observer in the United States, I have gained the impression that Americans in recent years have been more successful than Europeans in dealing with structural problems. Investment patterns have changed, and although the adjustment process has been very painful for a large number of people in various sectors of the economy, the needed structural changes have been taking place.

When I look now at Western Europe, I don't get the same feeling. On the contrary, as an Italian working for the Italian government on these matters, I have the very distinct impression that we are not yet beginning to tackle the basic problem of the low real return on both public and private investment. We have developed a number of devices—we Europeans are very inventive—to prop up the return on those investments artificially, but, from the standpoint of economic efficiency, such devices make little sense. The key problem is how to get out of this maze of propping-up gimmicks so that we can begin to readjust our economies.

Now this is something that, for the European economies, which are comparatively small and tightly knit with one another, is very difficult to do in isolation. At the same time, it is extremely difficult to develop a system of consultation, or exchange of information, for this type of policy, because we are dealing here with medium-term and long-term policies. And if, to quote our chairman, our policy-makers are in a mist when they talk about short-term policies and their reactions to them, they are in a much darker mist when they talk about longer-term policies. But, whether they like it or not, they are implementing some kind of medium-term and long-term policies even if they have no clear idea about their objectives. The issue is how to get these longer-term policies clarified, as well as internationally consistent with one another, in order to get the structural changes we need.

*Emminger*: May I first take up a remark which Mr. Vaubel made about central bank policies, because, as a former central banker, I found it rather provocative. If I understood him correctly, he implied that central banks are usually determined to expand the money supply until they reach a point were they are punished somehow by international competition. Now maybe I misunderstood him, but this is certainly not the way in which I know central banks to be working. He also made another interesting remark; he said that of course central bankers are interested in veiling, so to speak, the effect on prices of their expansionary policies, whereas they should be interested, he said, in seeing this effect immediately. Again, I would say that this is not the understanding I have of all the central bankers that I know. But it's a very interesting point, because I note that in several countries, especially in the United States but of late also in Germany, economists are doing everything they can to raise inflationary expectations by saying that any upward movement in the economy will immediately increase inflationary dangers.

Now, of course, anybody can say anything he likes, but this sort of talk is far from helpful in dealing with the problem, mentioned by Max Corden, of maintaining a continuing recovery. My hunch is that, because of such talk, governments and central banks will be under so much pressure from this crisis of expectations that they will very soon, even in the very first phase of recovery, step on the brakes— and much sooner than they otherwise would. That is why I expect a rather, I wouldn't say weak, but not a very good, sustained recovery. It will be a bumpy recovery and perhaps not vigorous enough to solve the problem we discussed yesterday afternoon—namely, the international debt problem.

Having made this remark, I may perhaps also make a remark on the actual situation which faces the Williamsburg summit conference. But, first of all, what is really holding back some countries from pursuing more expansionary policies? There has been a great deal said this morning about the effect of expansionary policies on the terms of trade. Now this is certainly something which is not unimportant, but I think the real world is a more primitive world. The French, for instance, had to draw back, not because they were concerned about a worsening of the terms of trade, but simply because of the adverse effect of their expansionary policies on their balance of payments on current account. So it's very primitive; it's the effect on the current account. But one could ask why countries that are not constrained by the current account do not expand on their own—for instance, the Japanese.

*Kaldor*: Or the British.

*Emminger*: Or the British; I was about to mention Mrs. Thatcher. Or the Germans, who, although not having a large current-account surplus, at least have no present worries about the current account; everyone says that the current-account surplus this year will be slightly larger than it was last year.

Now why don't these countries expand when they have no balance-of-payments constraint? The example of Germany has already been referred to by Dr. Matthes. I could add a great deal to what he said about the motives of the German government in not going in for a clearly expansionary policy, but I will discuss instead the example of Japan, because there was a very interesting conference two or three weeks ago in Tokyo, where we had an exchange of views with the leading Japanese industrialists and bankers. We also heard a brilliant paper by the chief economist of the Japanese government. This very able man explained to us why the Japanese at present are very averse to any expansionary policies.

First, he stated that Japan was in a recession, because when the rate of growth is only 1 or 2 percent, the Japanese consider themselves in a recession—and, from their point of view, quite rightly. He said that it was an inventory recession, not an investment-type recession. This inventory recession, he stated, will disappear by itself, and then there will be an upturn.

But this was not his main argument. His main argument was the long-term structural argument—the one which was mentioned a moment ago by Dr. Pennisi and which is also very relevant in the German case. He said that Japan has experienced an increase of the government share in the gross national product from 22 percent ten years ago to 34 percent now. This observation amused me a little; I said to myself, "I wish I had your worries," because the government share in the German GNP is now 50 percent. But he said that Japan has watched other countries, and has observed that if a country oversteps a certain point in this process, it gets into very serious political and social difficulties. Thus Japan prefers to be less expansive in order not to get into the situation which the Americans and the Germans are in. And, of course, from a Japanese point of view, he was right. He also mentioned the aging of the Japanese population; that is one of the major long-term structural problems which adds to the pressure toward a very much enlarged social-welfare state.

Thus some countries are so much influenced or impressed by their structural and medium-term problems that they assign a second place to the short-term problem of recession. This is what I referred to yesterday as the conflict between the short-term policy problem and the longer-term structural problem. That will be one of the major difficulties at the summit meeting later this month. Having said this, however, I join the others who stress that it is very important that the major countries exchange information on these matters, including information on their contingent reactions, and I therefore agree that a well-prepared summit meeting can be a very positive step.

*Kaldor*: You never mentioned to your Japanese friend that Japan spends nothing on defense, because that didn't fit into your picture.

*Emminger*: Well, I said I didn't want to go into details. There are many other details too.

*Cooper*: I'd just like to make one point, though, on the short run versus the long run, since a number of people have emphasized the rising share of government, including transfer payments, in GNP. One way to attempt to reconcile short-run expansion with the long-term structural problem of the increasing government share in GNP is the tack the Reagan administration has taken, which is to cut taxes. This provides warranted short-term expansion on the assumption that, in the long run, the cut in taxes will in fact put a squeeze on government expenditures. Thus, over time, the expansionist policy need not lead to a continued increase, and may lead to a decrease, in the government share in GNP. There are contradictions in the Reagan program, but the point is worth keeping in mind. Vaubel has a two-handed intervention.

*Vaubel*: A quickie, yes. I think you would agree, Dr. Emminger, that central banks, including the Bundesbank, do pay attention to the exchange rate. Now, in my view, the depreciation of a currency in the foreign-exchange market is exactly the punishment which currency competition—competition among money producers— imposes. In my opinion, this is the main advantage of a flexible exchange-rate system—that it permits such competition and such punishment.

*Emminger*: I would not entirely agree. The Bundesbank formerly had to pay attention to the exchange rate, but only as long as the high dollar rate threatened to be an inflationary factor. Once it was no longer an inflationary factor—and that has been the case since about the middle of 1982—the dollar rate ceased to be a source of much concern for the Bundesbank. But I don't want to go into the details again.

*Arndt*: Just a brief remark on the Reagan program, which the chairman referred to a moment ago. Here, I think, the policy mix between monetary and fiscal policy is crucial. I would argue that the reason we are all expecting at best a modest recovery in the United States is that the policy mix has been too tight on the monetary side and too loose on the fiscal side.

*Scharrer*: Speaking of recovery, I have a conceptual problem that puzzles me a bit. It has become conventional wisdom by now that recovery is to be brought about by increased private investment and that the resulting expansion is to be transformed into higher employment through real-wage restraint. Lord Kaldor may not agree with that, but I think I am correct in stating the present consensus among economists.

Now my puzzlement begins with the real-wage restraint. If we keep real wages constant—that is, if nominal wages are rising only enough to keep up with price increases—an entrepreneur may think that, on the cost side, he is in a favorable position; the wage increases he has to grant are matched by price increases. But if he looks at other firms, he sees that there is wage restraint all around, so he may ask himself where the demand will come from to buy the goods which he is supposed to produce with the expanded investment.

Thus the question is: Why should there be any additional investment? To make my own position clear, I am equally hesitant to say that a wage push would be the right answer, but I wonder whether real-wage restraint can lead to expansion in the world economy. Of course, the entrepreneur may look beyond the borders of his country, and say, "Well, my real costs are constant; I shall try to expand my sales in countries where real costs are rising. My competitive position in those countries will be improving, and I can increase my exports." But then he listens to the economists, who will tell him that the growth in exports will lead to a rise in the price of his country's currency in the exchange market, so that any initial competitive advantage may soon be lost—in six months, a year, or whatever the time is—in any case, a period too short to warrant new investment.

I wonder whether I am completely wrong and, if so, where the fallacy in my reasoning lies.

*Cooper*: Two people have promised answers: Jürgen Schröder and Max Corden.

*Schröder*: Perhaps my answer is too simple, but one way in which demand can increase is through the increased employment resulting from the increased investment; the newly employed will spend money that they formerly didn't have.

*Corden*: Let me give a list of where the extra demand would come from. First, as Professor Schröder said, there will be extra people employed, so, while you have a constant real wage per person, you have a bigger real-wage bill, and thus more real income and expenditure. Secondly, there will be the extra inventory investment which can be expected as part of the recovery. One reason we expect a recovery is because there has been a rundown in inventories, and

we need some private investment to correct that. Thirdly, if the recovery is created by monetary expansion, interest rates will be down,
and credit will become more available, so, even with constant expectations, we get more investment because credit is easier to obtain.

Now, the hitch in this reasoning—and the problem that Scharrer
is hinting at—is that I'm describing a new equilibrium situation in
which new investment is already taking place. But the question is:
How do we get there from here? And the answer is that, at some
point, entrepreneurs will have reason to expect that higher demand is
in the offing and that they will need to employ more people to meet
that higher demand. This will not be a smooth process; people will
feel their way slowly at various steps, but eventually the expansion
always does take place. So the basic answer is that we can have a
recovery with constant real-wage rates, because there will be more
spending out of profits, more spending on investment, and more
spending out of a higher wage bill. The mechanism of how you get
from here to there is the normal way in which the economy adjusts
to any change.

*Meade*: I would like to draw a distinction between the conventional wisdom and Wisdom. I am now going to represent Wisdom. I
want to make one very simple point, and that is to say that there is a
difference between the real-wage rate, or real-wage cost, to the employer and the income of the wage earner. My wisdom would be to
cut rates of tax to start the whole thing off; the whole thing would be
started off by the fact that, while wage costs have not gone up—and,
therefore, prices needn't go up—the incomes of all people, including
the wage earners, would be bigger. This would stimulate the demand
for consumption goods, and thus people would have a bigger incentive to invest. There would be a Keynesian multiplier, and we would
be in heaven.

*Scharrer*: That would be the case for a tax cut.

*Meade*: Yes, but the point I want to make is that there is a difference between the income of people and the costs which they impose
on price formation.

*Cooper*: But the tax cut provides the purchasing power, which
provides the demand for future investment. That's the chain of reasoning.

*Meade*: Yes, it provides the initial impulse. Whether the process
expands on its own momentum after that will depend on the parameters.

*Gutowski*: I just want to add to what Dr. Scharrer said about the
situation which Keynes referred to as unduly pessimistic expectations. Under such conditions, a stimulation of the demand process

would be appropriate. One way—and perhaps the best way—to do that would be through a tax cut. Another way would be through increased public expenditure.

*Matthes*: I would agree with Professor Gutowski. It seems to me that one principal obstacle to Professor Meade's case for a tax cut is what one might call the disappearance of fiscal illusion and the public acceptance of a budget deficit as nothing to be greatly concerned about.

*Meade*: Well, that's due to the nonsense that some economists have been preaching for so many years.

*Kaldor*: I may be talking bigger nonsense than anybody else, but I can see what may happen at the Williamsburg meeting—that each government will come forward with carefully collected arguments, saying, "World economic recovery is a wonderful thing, but our government can't be a locomotive; we can't initiate recovery, but when it happens it will be very good." And I'm afraid that the meeting will be just as big a washout as the previous meetings were.

Now we all know that, quantitatively, the most important cycle in the world economy in the 1970s and 1980s—but not the one most often talked about—is the very long cycle identified many years ago by the Russian economist Kondratrieff. This is a cycle of about fifty years, in which, with little variation, twenty-five good years—expansionary years—alternate with twenty-five bad years. I've thought a great deal about this and about what on earth can be the reason, as did Kondratieff when he published his article in 1921 and found that none of the obvious explanations would work. You cannot connect it with war and peace periods, because they don't fit; you cannot connect it with high or low food prices or raw-material prices, because these don't fit. Sometimes a boom period comes to an end because of overproduction. The typical case is 1929. From 1925 on in the United States, commodity stocks started to increase, but the continuance of the boom was enough to hold prices up, at the cost of sharply rising supplies. Then world trade collapsed, and of course the expectation that the boom would continue also collapsed. This caused a very, very rapid fall in prices. The remaining interwar years were years of depression in one sense or another.

Then, after the second world war, we had a very long boom of twenty-five years—from 1948 to 1973. We know that the transition periods from war to peace are not that long. Well, historically, that resembled nothing so much as the long boom of mid-Victorian prosperity, which ran from 1846 to 1873; 1873 was the key year, and that proved to be the case also in 1973. At the beginning of that year, I suggested to Peter Jay, who was economics editor of the *Times*, that 1973 might be a year of change. He was so amused by my observation that he wrote a long article the next day: Kondratrieff prophesies that 1973 is going to be a year of change—ha, ha, ha! He laughed about it, and thought the whole thing ridiculous. Yet that was the year of the Yom Kippur war, the OPEC cartel, and so on. But commodity prices started rising well before that; the warning signs were all there to see. Wages started rising rapidly in France after the 1968 uprising. In 1969, German wages rose in double-digit figures, and all over Europe there was a renewal of inflationary pressures.

Our chairman suggested to me the other day that this was all perfectly explicable as the result of a series of fortuitous circumstances, of which a bad Russian harvest was one. But it wasn't just grain; metal prices went up like mad after 1971. The OECD produced a striking graph which showed that the course of metal prices followed with an uncanny similarity the free-market price of gold. The gold price, which at first did not rise much after the abandonment of the Gold Pool in 1968, shot up from $50 or $55 to over $200 an ounce within eighteen months. And that coincided very much with what was happening to copper, tin, and other commodities—all rising in the same way.

What I wish to say is that a long boom creates a situation which brings it to an end. There is no doubt that, with a long period of full employment, labor gets much more powerful in relation to capital and management. That certainly happened in England, and I think it has happened elsewhere. Then inflation gets worse and, as it gets worse, people get fed up with it. So you get the extreme case of Britain, where triumph over inflation is absolutely the first priority; nothing must stand in the way. Because of the oil bonanza, which meant that we were no longer hemmed in by the balance of payments, we were at last in the situation of being able to expand, invest, modernize, and arrest our long decline, but this was the very situation in which we got a government which imposed severely deflationary budgets. As a result, we've jolly near wasted the unexpected heritage from the North Sea oil. We did nothing about it. Instead, it enabled us to run down the economy, to lose 13 or 14 percent of our share of world trade, to close down an awful lot of industries, to sell the equipment at low prices to the Americans so that the factories were literally emptied and demolished. All this, however, didn't call forth the kind of reaction by the British population which it would have called forth if it had happened ten years earlier, when the British were very keen on the advantages of growth and full employment. On the whole, the people now support Mrs. Thatcher; they support the idea that inflation rather than unemployment is the chief evil.

A Finnish economist published a study in which he showed that economic policy becomes very monetarist, and therefore deflationary, every fifty or sixty years; sound money becomes the overriding consideration. Everybody now talks about recovery, and we shall have a recovery, but it won't last long, and it won't be very big. It won't be nearly big enough to put us back on the path which we followed between 1948 and 1973. And that situation I see likely to continue for at least another ten or fifteen years. By that time, a new generation will come forth, and that generation will be far more concerned with growth and full employment.

Now why does the Kondratieff cycle last about fifty years—not longer, not shorter? The only reason I can think of is that the average length of a human generation is twenty-five years. There is one generation of people who, so to speak, are brought up to regard inflation as the biggest evil; then you have a downward Kondratieff phase. The next generation is brought up with the fear of not getting jobs; then you have an upward Kondratieff phase. And so it goes on. This, of course, is all very unsatisfactory; it is extremely primitive, and it doesn't make use of any of the highly sophisticated, precise ideas which our friend from the Kiel Institute mentioned this morning. But it seems to me that these things are likely to happen for no more fundamental reason than that there are waves of human psychology which change people's value judgments of what is regarded as of primary importance. Given the present psychology, one can think of fifty wonderful reasons for saying, "Our situation in Germany is quite special; we can't expand," or "Our situation in Japan is most unusual; other countries must take the initiative." And therefore I don't expect that efforts at coordinated expansion are likely to get very far in the future. I'm sorry I've taken so much time.

*Cooper:* No, it's very interesting. I think maybe we've found the solution to Max Corden's problem—that he should invite Lord Kaldor to Australia to deal with the wage-expectation problem in the future.

*Emminger:* He would of course reinforce that psychology.

*Matthes:* I just want to object to Lord Kaldor that his thesis about the Kondratieff cycle being about two times the average length of a human generation could empirically only be tested after Kondratieff had written his book—namely, from 1923 onward.

*Kaldor*: From 1923 onward is what I talked about; that's the whole point.

*Schröder*: I would like to support the case for international economic coordination by raising a point that hasn't been made about the terms-of-trade argument. Since we all know that nominal wage rates tend to be flexible upward but rigid downward, any change in the terms of trade—induced, for example, by unilateral economic expansion—is likely to result in an average rise in nominal wage rates and therefore in price inflation, because the wage rise is not matched by a corresponding rise in productivity. This situation can be avoided by coordinated expansion, as the terms of trade in that case would presumably not be affected.

*Kaldor*: But what about commodity prices? When the Korean War broke out, before the United States was in a position to spend a penny on rearmament, the index of commodity prices rose by 50 percent—without any increase in consumption. Now that is what you call inflationary expectations, and I assure you that since 1973 inflationary expectations have operated three times as powerfully as they did before. At the beginning of a recovery, commodity prices rise like mad, and then, when the recovery is nipped in the bud by fear of inflation, commodity prices go down like mad. They are a far more important factor than wages.

*Corden*: Could I get into this? I agree with Lord Kaldor that the commodity-price issue is very important and that we ought to prepare for a commodity boom if we do have this expansion. The implication I draw is that there is no way of avoiding it; governments ought to explain to people that it's inevitable. There will have to be a fall in real wages because of the rise in commodity prices. And we don't want nominal wages to rise at a rate that would squeeze profits; that's one more reason why we will have to live with some fall in real wages when there's an economic expansion. The commodity boom itself will benefit many developing countries, thus helping to solve the debt problem. It will also benefit one or two developed countries, but that's just a footnote.

*Cooper*: If I can intercede before we push this too far, keep in mind the commodities we're talking about. For most of the industrial countries, food prices are insulated from these world price movements, and in any case they are not the ones that are terribly sensitive to the recovery. We're talking about rubber prices, tin prices, nonferrous metal prices.

*Matthes*: What about oil?

*Cooper*: With a world capacity of thirteen million barrels a day, we're not going to get a big increase in oil prices. Oil prices are like steel prices; they're sluggish these days, they're not the sensitive prices. And it's not clear that there will be any change in the prices of finished products as a result of a rise in input prices. The effect, rather, is the psychological one, which is that basic commodity prices enter into the wholesale-price indexes, which will go up; the indexes are reported in newspapers, and attract immediate attention. But even though we may get a substantial increase in the prices of industrial materials, it is not clear, in the early stages of the recovery, that purchasers of final goods and services need feel any price effect. James:

*Meade*: I merely want to say the same thing that Max Corden said, but I will modify it with your very important footnote that it may not be quantitatively as important as he made out. But the implication is that insofar as this rise in commodity prices does affect the price of finished goods to the consumer, it reinforces the necessity for wage restraint. It may be that wage restraint is necessary on other grounds, as I will argue this afternoon, but Nicky's point reinforces the need for wage restraint.

*Kaldor*: But Mrs. Thatcher's method of wage restraint is different from yours.

*Meade*: I'm sorry, I'm not talking about Mrs. Thatcher.

*Kaldor*: She has a very effective policy of wage restraint.

*Meade*: I'm not talking about Mrs. Thatcher, Nicky. But the need for wage restraint is obvious if any policy of expansion, however it is brought about, is going to last. You, Mr. Chairman, suggest that perhaps Nicky and I, who agree on this, are exaggerating.

*Cooper*: I don't disagree with the qualitative point; I just think one should not fall into the habit of thinking of these commodities, whose prices are admittedly very sensitive to industrial activity, as behaving the same way as the finished goods that the man in the street buys. In their price behavior, they don't; that's all.

*Heller*: I would like to switch to two broad issues that seem to me important these days. One is macroeconomic and the other microeconomic.

I think the overriding macroeconomic fact of the day is that we are coming to the end of a period of inflation. The big question here is: What does this do to the demand for money? According to one estimate that I have seen, there would be a 15 percent increase in the demand for money when the rate of inflation drops to zero, because money in that situation becomes a much more attractive liquid asset to hold. This, of course, is a very important consideration in judging the correctness of monetary policy by, say, the Bundesbank or the Federal Reserve. The issue here is: Should those institutions continue to step on the brakes, thereby risking a new period of deflation, or should they accommodate the one-time increase in the demand for money by authorizing a corresponding increase in the supply? That's an empirical question of the utmost importance.

Let me now turn to my microeconomic point. I am thinking here of the illusion that we had during the 1960s—that we could afford everything. But all we have to do is to take a trip to Korea and see the Koreans working sixty or seventy hours a week at half the wages presently prevailing in Europe or in the United States to grasp the point that we cannot have all our present entitlements and transfer payments if we are to compete successfully with the newly industrialized countries. What we have to do is to increase our own productivity. And to do that we need new investment. The only way to get that new investment is to reduce real rates of interest. And, over the longer run, the only way to get real interest rates down is by increased saving. So we have to stop taxing dividends; we have to stop taxing capital gains. In the United States, we have made progress in this direction with the introduction of IRA accounts, but the nontaxation of saving clearly needs to be broadened. And, as a flanking operation to promote greater productivity, we need to reduce protectionism.

*Kaldor*: May I make two rapid corrections? In the first place, capital gains are not a source of savings. Secondly, we have long ago abandoned in all countries except the United States a tax on dividends, and in England we've even abandoned the tax on company profits. And it doesn't seem to make all that difference. A year or two ago, I was at Kiel at a conference. We were already in a recession, and the one thing the Kiel economists and I agreed on—it was the *only* thing we agreed on—was that Germany suffers from too much saving, not too little.

*Vaubel*: It doesn't.

*Kaldor*: It isn't a shortage of saving that's kept investment back; it's the lack of profit incentives, which the Kiel economists attributed to the fact that the share of wages had become too large, and the share of profits too small, in the national income—not realizing that the change in those shares was a reflection of the recession and not the cause of it. When you invest little, then profits will be low, and if profits are low, the share of wages will be high.

*Craven*: I've noted this morning that we've been scrupulously avoiding the form that the economic expansion is supposed to take.

We haven't been debating the pattern of the expansion; we've been talking about what will happen if we expand. But I don't think we should continue to dodge this question. What I'm concerned about is that we economists may be imputing to market participants our own perceptions of how the economy behaves. For instance, I don't know of any market participants in my country who think in terms of real income; they all think in terms of nominal income, and assume that the price effects of their actions will not affect them nearly as much as the direct nominal returns they hope to get. We economists properly analyze the real effects, but the market, I think, doesn't think in those terms.

In this connection, there is a danger that market participants, viewing a change in policy that they're unfamiliar with—such as a major tax cut—may react in such a way that, despite the fact that they have more net earnings, they sit on those earnings instead of spending them. In this case, the fact that earnings have increased doesn't generate the expansion we want. And I hardly need add that if expansion is achieved through a major increase in the budget deficit which sharply raises interest rates, it may be very short-lived.

*Kaldor*: I entirely agree with Howard Craven, as against other economists, that the labor market, for example, doesn't think in real terms. Workers, looking backward, take into account the rise in prices which has occurred since the last wage settlement. But they don't look forward; they're quite incapable of looking forward and of taking their expectations into account in determining their stance on wages. But inflationary expectations are very important in one field; they are important for professional speculators in commodity markets. In other words, inflationary expectations are important only in those fields where speculation is important—where the current price is very much under the influence of purely speculative purchases and sales. They're important in the stock exchange, and they're important in the commodity market, but they are not important in the labor market.

*Gutowski*: I completely disagree with Lord Kaldor that inflationary expectations don't play a role in wage settlements. Let me give an example. In 1974 in Germany, both employers and employees, because of the oil crisis, expected a sharp rise in the rate of inflation, and they reached a wage settlement involving double-digit rates of increase. At the same time, the Bundesbank had the distressing problem of deciding whether to accommodate the wage increase by a corresponding monetary expansion or to try to put an end to inflationary expectations. It decided to step on the brake. That meant that, in spite of the drastic oil-price increase, we had the same rate of inflation in 1974 as in 1973—a 7 percent rate in both years. But the increase in real wages was much greater than either side had expected or really wanted, because both sides had expected much higher inflation. And that was the root of our problem later, because the excessively high level of real wages produced our high level of unemployment.

So the German unions have had to learn the hard way that they have to take into account the terms-of-trade effect. But if a country like Germany has a deterioration in its terms of trade, and if the unions agree simply to hold the line on nominal wages, the question still arises whether the central bank should accommodate the situation by a once-and-for-all increase in the price level or whether, by restrictive monetary policy, it should try to force nominal wages down in order to preserve a stable price level and a level of real wages consistent both with that price level and with high employment.

J. E. Meade and
Members of the
Conference

# Proposals for a Better Economic Future

*Chairman Cooper*: Yesterday morning, we had a number of suggestions in the opening statements of changes that should be made in the way that the system as a whole—including the international monetary system—operates, so this afternoon we will focus on these longer-range, structural questions. First on my list is James Meade, who has some thoughts on these matters. James, the floor is yours.

*Meade*: I'd like to make two introductory remarks. The first is that I'm an old and pompous professor, given to lecturing, with a very slow mind now. I'm easily put off my train of thought, and I wonder if I could ask, Mr. Chairman, that people not interrupt me until I've stopped.

*Cooper*: Nicky, I'm looking at you.

*Kaldor*: Am I to be encouraged or discouraged?

*Cooper*: Let me put it positively; you are to be encouraged to hold your comments until after James has finished.

*Meade*: My second remark is that, having been, I think, reasonably silent during the previous sessions, could I be allowed to go on for a little bit of time—say, quarter of an hour? Would that be awful?

*Cooper*: That would be all right.

*Meade*: Very good. I would like to start with what Max Corden has said, because I agree that the basic economic problem of our society is wage-fixing. It may be that I'm too influenced by U.K. history, but I think that, although the institutional aspects differ from country to country, the problem is basically the same in Germany, in the United States, and in other countries. To put the matter directly, do we or do we not believe—to take an extreme case—that if there were an increase in economic activity which caused unemployment to drop, say, from 15 percent to 3 percent, there would be an outbreak of wage claims that were in excess of any conceivable increase in productivity?

I think we do believe this. My reason for believing it is based perhaps too much on the U.K. institutions, but let me put it this way. The trade unions are very strong in the United Kingdom, and are very uncoordinated in spite of the T.U.C.; they act rather independently in the different sectors. Now it is the function of a trade-union leader—and it's not an immoral function; it's what he's there for—to do the best he can for those of his members who are in employment. He may take some account, and members in employment may take some account, of members who have recently lost their jobs. And while a recession is taking place, members may be very restrained in their wage claims because of fear of pricing themselves out of a job. But as soon as expansion starts, the scenario changes, because if the people in employment and their representatives are interested in the best for those who are in employment, and are not considering the interests of the outsiders, then, when the demand for the product increases, and they have the option of allowing more workers to come in at the same wage or of raising the wage and getting more for themselves, I think the nature of trade-union organization is such as to lead to a good deal of emphasis on the second choice.

Now I think this is a basic problem. I know many people disagree with me, but I am not at all hopeful that, if we get an expansion, we shall not move again toward an explosive inflation. I'm not afraid of inflation; I'm afraid of *explosive* inflation—where claims for wage increases far exceed the increase of productivity. When that happens, you get explosive inflation. Now I don't want to talk about wage reform, because the problem obviously differs greatly from country to country, but I do believe that this matter of wage-fixing is of crucial importance. I think that wage reform does involve an enormous shift of opinion about the function of wage-fixing and that wage-fixing in the future must be considered much more as an instrument for providing full employment—employment for outsiders—and less as an instrument for giving to insiders a certain artificially high real income. I'm a strong egalitarian; I can offer ten hourly lectures, if you like, on this problem, but I will restrain myself and say no more about it.

But, supposing one holds this view, what, then, is the right sort of financial policy to adopt? The orthodox Keynesian would say that in a situation of this kind you should expand total demand by the whole panoply of Keynesian measures—monetary policy, fiscal policy, exchange-rate policy—to increase the demand for goods and services until we've gained something which I will call full employment—again I won't bother about exactly what that is—and to maintain demand at that necessary level. And if this leads to a wage-price explosive inflation, you should introduce some form of incomes policy which, by central control or influence, establishes the money-wage rate, not at a fixed level, but allows it to rise by 5 percent or 2 percent per annum, or whatever you think is a reasonable figure. Instead of fixing the price of gold or the price of a basket of commodities, or instead of maintaining M-1 or M-2 or M-3 on a steady growth path, you establish your incomes policy—the wage rate—as your monetary anchor.

Now I don't accept that; I think that it's not going to be possible, and I don't like it. I suggest that the best monetary anchor for the individual countries is to watch their nominal gross national product (or, more precisely, gross domestic product) and to design their financial policies—I won't say which yet—so as to keep the nominal GDP on a steady growth path; let me suggest 5 percent per annum. Now against this, it is then up to the wage-fixing reform to look after employment. If you know that the total money demand for the products of labor is going to rise by 5 percent per annum, then you can take that out either in increased employment or in increased wages per worker. But I'm not in favor of just leaving that—as I think Mrs. Thatcher is—to the trade unions; I think we've got to take positive reform measures.

Now this, I think, is a very much better monetary anchor target than M-1, M-2, or M-3. I was extremely interested in what Robert Heller said this morning. You never know when you look at the monetary figures whether, when the money supply goes up, it's because people have lost their fear of inflation and simply wish to hold more of their assets in the form of money or whether it's because monetary policy has been too expansionary and thus is causing an inflation. You never know. Heller says it's a very real problem; I say it's a very real problem, but don't worry about it. Don't watch M-1, M-2, or M-3; watch the nominal GDP. If that's going up too quickly, then you know that your financial policies should be more restrictive; if it's not going up enough, you know they should be less restrictive.

Now, supposing a single country were to adopt this GDP target, the next point I want to make is that the country must use fiscal policy rather than monetary policy for this purpose. And on a particular point in this connection, I've changed my mind; as one grows older, one grows wiser. I no longer believe that variable exchange rates will allow you to be thoughtless about what other countries are doing about their monetary policy in relation to your own monetary policy.

Being a good Keynesian, I like to put this in terms of interest rates rather than in supplies of money.

Let me take a very simple and extreme example. Suppose the short-term nominal rate of interest—say, on Treasury bills or on whatever you think is the right measure of a riskless rate—is 15 percent in the U.S.A., while we in the U.K. want it at 5 percent because we've got Keynes in power rather than Mrs. Thatcher, and we're trying to expand. If we expect that discrepancy to go on for three years, or people in the market do, then the natural thing would be for the pound sterling to depreciate until it was 30 percent below what one might call a purchasing-power parity, because for three years you must expect the exchange to appreciate by 10 percent per annum to make up for the interest difference. In other words, if you really try to use monetary policy for this purpose, I think you'll get horrific overshooting or undershooting of the exchange rate if you leave it free.

Now if you turn to fiscal policy, there is one point that I want to make very clear. If you are using tax cuts to maintain your nominal GDP at an appropriate growth rate, this does not necessarily mean that you are increasing the public sector of the real economy. I want to stress this; there is nothing in the nature of things why you shouldn't be cutting real public-sector expenditure at the same time that you're cutting taxes *more* than you're cutting real expenditure— and therefore getting a fiscal boost. So the two things are quite separate in my view. When I say fiscal policy, I mean it in this sense. It does of course lead to a bigger budget deficit while it's on, but it need not lead to a bigger structural deficit.

Well now, suppose a country were to do this alone. I have been working with a model-building economist from Australia and a control engineer from the department of engineering in Cambridge, and, on the basis of our dynamic model, we have tried to see what would happen in the U.K. if, instead of Mrs. Thatcher, we had put in power John Maynard Keynes—no, not Keynes, but James Edward Meade, because I'm not quite sure what Keynes would be saying. Now the story is not unexpected, but it is very clear-cut. There is a world depression, and we in the U.K. decide not to have it. The main effect of the world depression is, of course, to reduce the demand for our exports; our GDP is no longer sustained at its steady growth path, so we reduce taxes. The reduction of taxes mainly affects consumption, but it maintains imports while exports fall, and it has a threefold effect. For one thing, there is a movement of the terms of trade against the U.K. When the world depression takes place, we have to depreciate the real rate of exchange in order to expand our exports of manufactures into the markets of those who are going to enjoy the depression without doing anything about it. And this turns the terms of trade against us. But, given the parameters of our model, that does not, on balance, make us worse off; the adverse change in the terms of trade takes away a substantial part of the gain in real income resulting from the tax cut, but does not take away all of it.

But there remain two very difficult results. The model suggests that there is a very considerable lag in the response of world markets to the lower price (in terms of foreign currencies) of our exports. The balance of payments returns to balance after two years, but during these two years there is a horrific strain on the balance of payments; I call it our "horror story." We end up with an enormous indebtedness to the IMF or to the Germans or to somebody; it depends on who will finance us during this period—we've assumed somebody would. But we also end up with a very big increase in the national debt and, of course, a very big increase in the interest burden on that debt. So when the thing is over and we don't have to rely on these tax cuts any longer, we're left with a large part of the gain absorbed by the terms of trade and another large part absorbed by the owners of the new debt.

Now what could we do about it? There are three—well, I suppose there are four—things that can be done. One is to give up this policy, but we British bulldogs would be very unwilling to do that, so I'll leave that out. A second alternative is to ride it out, and that may be the right way to go about it, but it does mean that with these time lags—which may be exaggerated—there's got to be an immense financing of the payments deficit for this period. A third possibility is to restrict imports, and that deals with both problems. As we expand or maintain demand, we shift it from imports onto home products to the same extent that foreigners reduce their demand for our exports, so we don't need the tax cut, or the same amount of tax cut, to maintain demand. And we don't have a balance-of-payments deficit.

Well now, I suppose I'm very arrogant—I don't always display it, but I'm going to display it now—I think I can claim to being one of the two founding fathers of the General Agreement on Tariffs and Trade, and I negotiated a large part of it on behalf of the United Kingdom. I think I drafted the Article on the use of import restrictions on balance-of-payments grounds. And I certainly had Keynes breathing down my shoulder—not literally, of course. Under the GATT Article, we would be perfectly justified in imposing import restrictions in this instance; that is the whole point of the Article. If the rest of the

world will have a depression and we won't, then we're entirely justified; we're not doing anybody any harm—it's they who are harming
themselves. We're just not bailing them out by maintaining the demand for their goods if they reduce their demand for our goods.

But I'm strongly against the use of this instrument, not because I
don't think it has a justification on macroeconomic grounds during
this period, but because, although I'm a very academic chap, I am sufficiently aware of the real world to realize that if the U.K. went in for
an extensive policy of import restriction, that would be the end, I
suspect, of the commercial-policy attempt toward freer trade.

So there is only one thing left—to get other countries to behave
sensibly as well as ourselves. And that is called coordination. Some
call it by other names, but I call it coordination, and that is what the
situation requires.

Now what form should this coordination take? I'm not talking
about Williamsburg now or about next year, because a lot of educa-
tion is necessary before one gets onto this. I would like the following
system; I think it could be built up with a limited group of countries,
or with the whole lot—which of course is what I would like to see. I
would like to see a world in which the national governments were
responsible both for setting their own nominal GDP targets, which
they would seek to maintain by their own brand of fiscal regulator,
and for establishing their own wage-fixing arrangements and reforms,
which would either result in full employment or in enough unemployment to be compatible with their GDP targets. All that, I think,
is domestic, and I'm strongly in favor of making domestic as much of
the program as possible. That is not to say, of course, that it wouldn't
be very useful to have international discussion and exchange of information, particularly about the GDP targets that were being thought
of in each country, but my point is that these would be basically domestic decisions.

But I do believe that as far as interest rates, exchange rates, and
the use of foreign-exchange reserves in official financing are concerned, one does need more. One needs international decisions and
obligations. Now I'm just going to reel off, in five rules, what I think
the new Bretton Woods principles might be on these lines. They're
not at all detailed, and, for lack of time, I shall just state them very
dogmatically.

I think the first thing that this group of countries would have to
do would be to agree on what I would call real exchange-rate targets.
I won't call them purchasing-power parities, because I don't like the
word parity; it leaves out the terms of trade. The question here is

how each country should adjust its nominal exchange rate in order to maintain a given agreed degree of competitiveness for its own exports relatively to the similar goods in other countries. Now this would require a great deal of sophisticated thought as to how these real exchange rates should be measured and how they should be consistent. But that would be the first general principle.

Now the second principle, I would say, is that there then should be agreement on an interest-rate structure, which in the first instance would determine, not the absolute levels, but the *difference* between the interest rates in the various countries, these differentials being so devised as to affect international capital movements in a way that would help to preserve the agreed real exchange rates with a minimum of intervention from foreign-exchange reserves. I know this all sounds awfully airy-fairy and undetailed, but I am limiting myself to enumerating the principles.

The third principle would relate to the absolute level of this structure of interest rates. Now it's here that there is, I think, a very interesting criterion under such a system. It's quite clear that the whole structure should be brought down if, throughout this group of countries (I'm thinking of the OECD countries, to start with), it was found that governments were having to rely on excessive budget deficits to maintain their nominal GDPs. That would be a signal that the whole structure of interest rates should be brought down, thereby stimulating private investment and expenditure through monetary policy rather than through this national regulator of fiscal policy. So now we've taken care of real exchange rates, relative interest rates, and absolute interest rates.

My fourth principle concerns what we should do when, as obviously will be the case from time to time, it appears necessary to change the real exchange rate. What should influence that? If we find that there is one country which is having great difficulty in maintaining its GDP, and is having to have an excessive budget deficit to do so, while another country is in the opposite position of having to have a big budget surplus to prevent its GDP from exploding, then that is the time when the real exchange rate of the first country should be depreciated in terms of the real exchange rate of the second country. That will expand the demand for the goods of the budget-deficit country, so that the tax rate can then be restored, and will contract the demand for the goods of the budget-surplus country, which can then cut taxes. At the same time, the relative interest rate can be altered, because the current-account position of the budget-deficit country—after the lag I mentioned—will be improved, while the current-account position of the budget-surplus country will be reduced. There will be less need on capital account to attract funds to the budget-deficit country from the budget-surplus country, and therefore the interest rate can be reduced a little in the former and raised a little in the latter. That will help by stimulating domestic investment in the budget-deficit country and restricting it in the budget-surplus country, which in turn will help to improve the budget position of both countries.

My fifth and last principle deals with the lag between the change in the real exchange rate and the desired effect on the balance of trade. The first effect of the altered exchange rate is to make the balance-of-payments problem worse, not better. In order to prevent a perverse rise in interest rates in the country with a budget-deficit problem, this is above all the period in which there should be official financing of the country's current-account deficit while the change in the real exchange rate is having its full effect.

These, then, are the principles. They may sound very academic, but I'm not as unaware of the real world as I may appear to be. For lack of time, I've had to put all this very crisply, and I don't think it's quite as easy as I've made out. That's all I've got to say.

*Cooper*: Thank you very much. So this is a regime for management of economic relations among like-minded nations, in some sense.

*Meade*: Yes, with basically a GDP target instead of an M, or monetary, target.

*Cooper*: Yes. Who would like to comment? Bob Mundell:

*Mundell*: I think it's completely unrealistic. I don't believe that you can talk about real exchange rates or real interest rates in any sense that is at all negotiable when we don't know what these real rates are. We don't know what a real interest rate is, because that involves expectations about future prices and interest rates. We can only know these ex post. If you framed everything in terms of monetary rates minus expected rates of inflation, then you'd have to decide how you would determine what those expected rates of inflation are.

*Corden*: I think some of us may be a little stunned by the complexity of this all. As a former student of Professor Meade, I must say that my experience has been: He's always right. One may not understand his reasoning, one may need a week to think about it, but finally it will turn out to be right, and that's the presumption on which we should now analyze his proposal. As for me, I'm struggling to see its significance and to translate it into terms that may be more familiar to me now, even though I was once his student.

Let me try to reinterpret what I think are some of the elements of the model. Suppose we have a system of managing exchange rates in which we don't have fixed nominal rates; instead, central banks intervene in the foreign-exchange market in order to maintain fixed real rates of exchange. The real rate is not permitted to vary with capital movements, so we are dealing with a fixed-rate system, but of real rather than nominal rates. Now I think we know from the Mundell-Fleming model that if we have fixed exchange rates and perfect capital mobility, then we're going to have unified interest rates— leaving aside expectations for the moment. In effect, what we have is monetary policy targeted on the exchange-rate requirement, and we have fiscal policy targeted on internal balance. To summarize, what we have in the Meade proposal is a fixed real exchange-rate system, with monetary policy then determined by this system and with internal balance maintained by fiscal policy.

Now what happens to the current account in this situation? Well, at the given interest rate—I'm thinking in small-country terms before raising the issue of coordination—the private sector will have a certain level of investment and a certain level of saving, and that will provide one element of the current account—namely, that which is associated with the private-sector deficit or surplus. The other element, of course, is the public-sector deficit or surplus. The public-sector balance will vary in accordance with internal-balance requirements, and, when added to the private-sector balance, will give us the overall current-account position in the balance of payments. Thus, at a time when the budget deficit is increased to maintain employment, there will be a concomitant increase in the deficit on current account.

The way I've told the story is in terms of a small-country model. But there is also the question of thinking about these matters for the system as a whole. One way of doing this is to think of the United States as the residual and of every other country as a small country, each intervening in the foreign-exchange market to maintain the real exchange rate it wants. In this context, I think, international coordination becomes relevant if we form a view, as we did yesterday, about desirable interest rates; we were saying that the world interest rate is too high, and so we were urging the United States to reduce its budget deficit. The alternative is to take a decentralization approach, à la Vaubel. We could simply allow each country to make its own decisions with regard to budget deficits and surpluses—its own judgment of internal-balance requirements—and allow the world interest rate to come out in the wash. That rate would then be regarded as the equilibrium rate—the result of all the decentralized decisions.

*Matthes*: I have a question, Professor Meade, with regard to your nominal GDP target. As I understood you, you don't want to accommodate the slack. That means that you only accommodate capacity rates of growth. Have I understood you correctly?

*Meade*: I'm sorry, I didn't understand.

*Matthes*: I mean you accommodate the capacity rate of growth and not the actual rate of growth. Is your concept capacity-oriented in this sense?

*Meade*: Well, I think one could do as one wanted in different countries, but I thought of it myself as a growth rate of a reasonably low kind—say, 5 percent per annum—in the nominal national income.

*Matthes*: That would be a capacity-oriented concept.

*Meade*: Yes. It would then be for the other institutions and decision-makers within the economy to take out what they would take out. I think the basic problem of our society is to find a way of taking out in increased output—in capacity output—rather than in sufficient unemployment to prevent a rise in prices. That seems to me to be the basic problem; my proposals are merely the financial framework in which one might attack the problem in a way in which countries could cooperate.

*Matthes*: If you don't accommodate the slack and if you see the problem as capacity-oriented, I personally have no intellectual difficulties in switching from our central bank money target to a nominal GDP target.

*Meade*: How enormously encouraged I am, because you can now tell Heller that the problem which he said was basically important has no importance whatsoever!

*Matthes*: Well, it has, after all, some importance.

*Meade*: You needn't look at it.

*Matthes*: I said that, intellectually, I had no problems; practically speaking, there are a lot of problems, of course.

*Meade*: Well, that's because we've stoked up such frightfully silly expectations of inflation whenever M goes up, even if that simply means that people just want to hold more money rather than other assets for very good reasons—possibly because they think inflation is going to be less. But as soon as they think inflation is going to be less and they decide to hold more money, they are told by all the financial journalists, stoked up by a lot of monetarists, that this will lead to inflation. And that's an absurd situation. I think we should try to persuade people to take their minds off M-1, M-2, and M-3, and look at the nominal GDP.

*Matthes*: But the acts of policy of the Bundesbank, for example, operating within a prearranged "corridor," imply much more discretionary power than a nominal GDP target.

*Meade*: Well, you might have a corridor for the GDP.

*Matthes*: It becomes difficult.

*Meade*: I don't want it.

*Hinshaw*: I'm very intrigued by the Meade program, and I would just like to think of it for a moment in a closed-economy context, which is the simplest way of looking at it. You [Meade] want money income to grow at an appropriate rate, whatever that is. Presumably, that would be determined by output per worker and by the growth in the working population—something like that. Well, whatever the appropriate rate is, that in itself, of course, does not assure either full employment or price stability; that you get with your wage proposals.

*Meade*: Yes.

*Hinshaw*: And if your wage proposals work out right, you get both price stability and full employment. My only other comment is that it would seem to me more difficult to get a steady growth in money income, or nominal GDP, than in, say, the monetary base, though I agree that money income is a more appropriate target.

*Cooper*: That's a little like saying that we should look for the keys under the light, because that's where the light is, even though the keys are someplace else. I mean that the monetary base is not our ultimate objective.

*Hinshaw*: Yes, but I do think there are real difficulties in achieving an appropriate and steady growth of nominal GDP, because what you're doing is looking at something that's already happened and trying to decide how you're going to jack that up by $X$ percent during the next year—then perhaps finding out that, despite your best efforts, what happens in the next year is wide of the mark.

*Meade*: Let me try to answer the questions which Randall raises, as I think they are very important ones. The first thing I want to make clear—and most of you may be shocked when I say this—is that I am not frightened by inflation. That is why I am very careless about what I say is the proper GDP rate of growth. Make the target 10 percent, perhaps, if you like. I don't like inflation, but I'm not terrified by it. But I am terrified by an explosive inflation. What frightens me is a situation where, if you have full employment, people insist on wage increases which are in excess of what's available, as determined by productivity. Then, if you maintain full employment, you get an explosive inflation. And therefore my first answer to Randall is that I'm not really terribly concerned about what rate of growth for nominal GDP is settled on, although I say 5 percent; I think that's reasonable. A 5 percent growth rate may mean that if you have a 2 percent growth in productivity, then, with full employment, you'll have a 3 percent rise in the price level. I'm not frightened by that; I'm frightened by an explosive inflation. That's the first point.

The second point, which of course is absolutely essential, is whether the dynamic interrelationships in the economy are such that you can control total expenditure. Milton Friedman often argues that you'll only make things worse. Well, in this connection we have carried out a very definite and detailed inquiry, to which I have already referred. And we say that you can control total expenditure, but you've got to call in your control engineers and do it properly. This isn't a problem that you can just brush under the rug, because the economy is full of lags, acceleration principles, and God knows what. But we have looked at these lags, at the administrative difficulties of altering tax rates frequently, and so on, though I don't want to pretend that the problem is an easy one.

*Corden*: Let me comment on some of the implications. The nominal GDP target in one respect has something in common with the old monetarist approach. It's a way of refusing to ratify nominal wage increases, so the basic philosophy is one of discipline on the labor market. Whether it's M-1, M-2, M-3, or MV is really just a matter of degree. In this respect, the nominal GDP is just a version of monetarism. On the other hand, the target involves a great deal of fine-tuning, and therefore will often be missed in the short run. Only after the event can you judge whether you are on target, so in this sense it's a Keynesian type of policy. To get MV (equal to money income) on target, you have to look at interest rates, M-1, M-2, and everything; and then, looking backward, you see whether you've got it right; if not, you take compensatory action. The basic idea is that, if you were off target, you are sending a signal to workers that you are taking steps to correct the situation, so they are not to think that the previous temporary overshooting is any kind of message for them to push up their wages. In this respect, I think the fundamental philosophy is that of monetarism. But it overcomes a major weakness of monetarism; there is no need to be concerned about the meaning of M.

*Matthes*: I think the difficult thing about the nominal GDP target is that M is an intermediate aim and that GDP is a final aim.

And it makes a great deal of difference whether the central bank aims at the intermediate target or at the final target. For example, in the latter case, the central bank is put in the position of having direct responsibility for giving wage guidelines, and that is a very difficult position for a central bank. Intellectually, I have no difficulty with the argument of Professor Meade, but, from a pragmatic point of view, I think that the nominal GDP target puts the central bank in a very uncomfortable position.

*Cooper:* I'm not sure I understand that; maybe you could enlighten us. Why is it more uncomfortable for a central bank like the Bundesbank or the Federal Reserve to be told to target nominal GDP—or MV, as Max Corden puts it—rather than to target central bank money, in the case of the Bundesbank, or M-1 or M-2, in the case of the Federal Reserve?

*Matthes:* Well, you see, in the derivation of the German monetary target, our point of departure is capacity rates of growth; we increase capacity rates of growth of GDP by a warranted price increase, and we then translate that into a CBM target. This is very different from attempting to aim directly at a nominal GDP, or MV, target.

*Kaldor:* What is a CBM target?

*Cooper:* CBM refers to central bank money; in other words, base money—the monetary base. I would like to change the subject and turn to the Meade exchange-rate proposals. If I understand you [Meade] correctly, the changes in real exchange rates that will take place from time to time under your regime would change real wages, and they would do that because you've got nominal wages under control. So you are assuming that your wage-control mechanism is sufficiently strong so that what Mundell and others call "money illusion" takes place. That's a very strong assumption.

*Meade:* It's a very strong assumption. It's the basic problem in our society.

*Cooper:* Yes. As I understand it, the changes in real exchange rates would be negotiated ones—negotiated in response, basically, to divergences in macroeconomic activity. Your example was a recession in the rest of the world, while you want to maintain full employment in your country. I would have thought that, although that kind of disturbance has certainly been very important over the last fifteen years, it has been by no means the only kind of disturbance to national economies; there are other reasons than cyclical divergences for changing real exchange rates, and that is one of the merits of the flexible exchange-rate system that we've had. That system has had many disadvantages, but one of its merits is that it has provided a

kind of shock absorber for disturbances coming from many directions, including supply-side shocks as well as demand-side shocks.

So let me ask some questions, which you may respond to later if
you wish. Is your scheme really a regime of fixed exchange rates—
fixed real exchange rates—the changes in which must be negotiated
to deal with disturbances from any quarter, or are we to ride out supply-side shocks? How would you deal with supply-side shocks? And
if it is a system of fixed, but adjustable, real exchange rates, isn't it
really a Bretton Woods in real terms rather than in nominal terms?
How do you deal with the problem of Bretton Woods, which was that
the anticipation of changes in exchange rates led to enormous movements of capital?

But maybe I've misunderstood the exchange-rate part of your proposal. It seems to me a critical part and, if I may say so, unviable. But
I may have missed something. You can comment on this later.

*Arndt*: Professor Meade, you have rejected incomes policy. Am I
correct in understanding that it's wage or labor-market discipline,
somehow brought about, that will control money wages? That's one
question. My other question is: What sorts of instruments are you using to manage exchange rates? You said you didn't want to specify
the mix of fiscal and monetary policy, but it seems to me you have
to. You want to manage real interest rates, you want to manage real
exchange rates, and you've got to worry about nominal wage rates.
Perhaps you could spend a moment and detail the kinds of instruments that you're bringing to bear on these targets.

*Meade*: Should I go through the comments so far?

*Cooper*: Yes.

*Meade*: I know I've not put the thing very clearly, and one of the
reasons is that it's not perhaps very clear in my own mind. I think
there are many alternative possibilities at different stages of my
structure, and I probably haven't specified them very clearly.

The first thing I would like to say is that I am not suggesting, as
Mundell interpreted me, that there should be any attempt to set real
interest rates in the sense of nominal rates plus some expectation of
inflation. I am suggesting that it is a matter for international discussion and decision what the structure of relative nominal exchange
rates should be, with a view to revising the nominal rates frequently
in such a way as to prevent the real exchange rates from diverging
too much from some agreed pattern of targetry. And I think that this
is meant to cover also Cooper's main point, of which I am very conscious, having, as he may remember, preached against what I call the
variable peg.

I think I should put it this way: The powers that be, the philosopher kings, who were getting together should have an idea of what would be a reasonable structure of some sort of purchasing-power parities, taking into account all kinds of shocks, and then they should try to set a structure of nominal exchange rates which, in their best judgment, given the way markets were behaving, would keep capital flows such as to reach these targets. That would be a basic regime of adjustable exchange rates, but it would be the change in the interest-rate structure which might control it.

*Cooper*: How would the real exchange rates get changed? By agreement?

*Meade*: By agreement. The authorities might say, "Well, this is a time when we ought to alter the structure of relative interest rates, because we want to alter the structure of exchange rates."

*Cooper*: Real exchange rates?

*Meade*: Yes. Unless we alter relative interest rates, the real exchange rates will remain much the same, and we want to alter those a bit.

*Cooper*: Bob Mundell wants to say something.

*Mundell*: I think this whole approach is wrong. I just don't see this as a field that negotiators would be any good at working in. Negotiators would seldom agree on how exchange rates should be altered and, when they did agree, I think that most of the time they'd be wrong; they'd move things in the wrong direction and increase the distortions.

Consider for a moment the yen-dollar rate. Earlier this year, the yen exchanged for the dollar at a rate of 278. Before that, it had been 170, then 220—when most people who were trying to calculate the real exchange rate said that the yen was undervalued. Nevertheless, it continued on to 278—in the opposite direction to what people who were making long-term forecasts were thinking. Since the beginning of this year, the yen quickly appreciated to 220 to the dollar, then depreciated again.

My point is that we haven't found ways of forecasting these rates; we can't distinguish between the equilibrium short-term rate and the equilibrium long-term rate. When exchange rates are negotiable, and when negotiators try to work in terms of the real exchange rate—which for me is a fictitious concept—we're moving from the frying pan we're in now into an inferno—Meade's inferno. Meade's proposals would create even more chaos than we already have, because he would add to all the present uncertainties a new form of uncertainty injected by the exchange-rate negotiators, each of whom would have his own theories about what a real exchange rate is and about how it should move. I mean, good heavens, Beryl Sprinkel would have a very different exchange-rate target for the pound than you or anybody else would, except perhaps a colleague in the administration. And he probably would do the wrong thing most of the time. At least the market does the wrong thing, if it does, only about half the time. And the best solution is to make the world economy more like the single national-currency economy, as was the case, more or less, under Bretton Woods or under the earlier gold standard, where the monetary rule, so to speak, was to maintain the exchange rate and to make that rate an equilibrium rate.

*Meade*: I just want to make the remark that we all agree, don't we, that at a certain point of time there was an absurd overvaluation of the pound sterling and that this was not unconnected with interest rates and monetary policy (I'm trying to hang out a calming thought to Bob Mundell). Or take the yen exchange rate; I've always been told, although I'm not very good at these grubby real things, that part of the yen undervaluation was due to the fact that the rate of interest in the United States was very high. The yen rate is not unaffected by the structure of relative interest rates, and I want to emphasize that I am not controlling the exchange rate; I am trying to get agreement on relative interest rates—on monetary policy. When you ask whether we want lower interest rates in the United States compared with Japan, I'm saying that the main thing you should look at is the real rate of exchange. Now I should have thought that the real exchange rate was terribly out of line in Japan at one time and terribly out of line in the U.K. at one time, and this leads me to the point that Dr. Matthes was raising—a point which I allowed him to get wrong. I think it is not the central bank that should be looking after the nominal GDP; the central bank should be looking after the interest rate and the rate of exchange. It would be the budget that would be looking after the GDP.

*Mundell*: But which should the central bank look after—the interest rate or the rate of exchange? It can only do one.

*Meade*: Well, it looks after the interest rate as an instrument for looking after the real exchange rate.

*Mundell*: It can't look after the *real* exchange rate.

*Meade*: It can look at the real exchange rate and say, "This is too high; put the interest rate down." If I were a central banker, I'd fill a buffer stock with D-marks and other currencies, and I would offer to buy and sell Treasury bills at a given price. When I looked at the price, I would ask, "Well, what has happened to the real exchange rate? Is it miles out of line with the purchasing-power rate?" And I would have conferred with my colleagues in the other governments and central banks regarding a reasonable structure of real exchange rates.

*Cooper*: So we have a rate of monetary growth for the system as a whole which either is a mutually agreed one or is given by the United States or some other big country, and then the other countries focus, not on the rate of monetary growth, but on this combination of exchange rates and interest rates.

*Meade*: That's right.

*Cooper*: And it's the budget authorities who look after the nominal GDP.

*Meade*: That's right. When I said that I wasn't going to talk about instruments, all I meant was that, for the time being, I wasn't going to talk about them. And I ruled out incomes policy only in the sense of a centralized fixing of wage rates. Actually, I require what I call a reform of wage-fixing institutions of a very severe kind, but I haven't talked about that. My monetary policy I define in terms of the rate of interest and not in terms of the money supply; I define monetary policy in terms of the domestic interest rate, and that I put up and down to look after the real exchange rate. So the interest rate looks after the real exchange rate, which looks after the balance of payments on current account and which can be changed by agreement. And the chancellor of the Exchequer or minister of finance is looking after the GDP. That is broadly what I'm saying.

*Gutowski*: If you fix the real exchange rate through negotiation and you then have capital flows brought about, let's say, by the public having a different risk assessment from that held by the government, wouldn't that require a great deal of intervention in the foreign-exchange market? The government would be saying, in effect, "Our official assessment is correct, given the policies being pursued and negotiated with other governments. In the meantime, the central bank is in a position to borrow foreign currencies, and this makes it possible for those who differ with the official risk assessment to move out of our currency." Am I right in this interpretation? Wouldn't this mean that there would have to be an enormous amount of central bank intervention?

*Meade*: Yes, I know, this is not a detail; it's a very basic point. But you can deal with it in more than one way within the general structure that I've tried to outline. In situations of this kind, you can have an agreement about immense amounts of official finance—and I'm rather in favor of that—or you can let the exchange rate go for a time. These are both possible, or some combination of the two. And I'm trying not to be dogmatic on this; that's partly why I've confused the discussion so. What I'm saying—and repeating—is that, the world being what it is, it's impossible to fix your exchange rate and your monetary policy at all sensibly as the main control of your domestic expansion or contraction; you've got to shift to fiscal policy for that. This is an essential point.

*Gutowski*: The way you handle this must have an impact on current-account balances.

*Meade*: Yes, undoubtedly. And you've got to take that into account, because, in my system, you have to balance the effect of the current account on inflation or deflation by a corresponding deflation or inflation through fiscal policy.

*Kaldor*: You are aiming at exchange rates by international agreement in real terms which will bring about zero balances of payments on current account—or something like that?

*Meade*: Well, which will enable you to run a balanced budget.

*Kaldor*: A balanced budget?

*Meade*: A balanced budget. That's the point which is so obvious and which people don't see.

Let me put it this way. Suppose we get into what I call our horror story in the U.K. because we've had Maynard Keynes and not Maggie Thatcher. We have a large budget deficit, because we're maintaining demand through cutting taxes, and we have a large current-account deficit in the balance of payments. And suppose we get stuck in that position. We then depreciate the exchange rate—the real exchange rate. The current-account balance will get worse for a period, but will then improve, and we will have stimulated foreign and domestic investment without changing the rate of interest. It's the optimal policy, because we will have depreciated the exchange rate sufficiently to expand the current account sufficiently to enable us to raise our taxes and remove the budget deficit. But we can now reduce the rate of interest, because we don't have to attract so many funds from abroad. We have more domestic investment and more foreign investment, both taking place at the same reduced rate of interest. So when we've got a budget deficit which is keeping employment up by subsidizing consumption, we can turn the situation right by stimulating foreign and domestic investment at the same rate of interest. It's a lovely system.

*Arndt*: I think I understand the system and its loveliness somewhat better than I did a minute ago, but let me just show you how well I understand it. Is it correct to say that if you could get the kind of discipline in the labor market that you need, you could—in consultation with other countries—then get, most of the time, the real exchange rate you want, by eliminating a lot of the pressures that move real exchange rates around in the short run, thus taking the burden off the interest rate and monetary policy? Is it a question of discipline?

*Meade*: If you want to end up without an explosive inflation and with full employment—which I won't define, but a much higher level of employment than we have at the moment—then I'm sure that this depends on what you call discipline in wage-fixing. That I'm absolutely certain of, and I think it's a basic problem. But what I've tried to outline as an *international* system is one where you leave success in that policy to the national governments. So each country is trying to keep its nominal GDP on a growth path of its own choice; its success on the wage front will determine whether that growth rate will be compatible with full employment or not. That is a domestic problem, and it's the same domestic problem whether you have M-1, M-2, M-3, MV, or anything else as your target.

*Kaldor*: Am I right in interpreting that you have some effective machinery, unspecified, which regulates domestic wages in such a way that the value of money, in terms of the domestic price level expressed in domestic currency, remains unchanged, regardless of changes in exchange rates or in interest rates?

*Cooper*: If I can reinterpret what Meade said, I believe he would regulate wages in a way that holds the money value of domestic *costs* constant, but the domestic money value of imports would vary with the exchange rate.

*Kaldor*: Oh, yes, I'm sorry—the price level of *value-added*, not the price level of final goods; the price level of value-added is the only thing you can regulate. To rephrase: The price level of value-added is kept constant by an effective wage regulatory mechanism. Now, having got this fixed point in the system—a stable value of money in this specific well-defined sense—you then manipulate your two instruments, the exchange rate and the interest rate, in such a way as to maintain either a foreign balanced position or, if your target is to be a capital exporter, then a corresponding surplus on current account or, if your target is to be a capital importer, then a targeted deficit on current account.

*Meade*: I wouldn't put it in terms of targets; if market relations are such that you ought to be a capital exporter, then you will be a capital exporter.

*Kaldor*: Well, how do you know that?

*Meade*: Simply by carrying out my rules.

*Kaldor*: The exchange rate and the interest rate won't give you enough information.

*Cooper*: The target, as I understand it, is the long-run budget position.

*Meade*: And I'll call that a budget balance. But it may be a surplus or a deficit, because you may target a surplus or a deficit. For example, you may decide that the government ought to save, because the private sector isn't saving enough. But if you are having to run a budget deficit that you don't want to run year after year, then you are in a situation in which you've got too little growth, too little investment, and too much consumption. You want to change that, and the way to do it is to increase investment. Now, as a good market chap, I say that it doesn't matter whether it's home investment or foreign investment in the sense of a current-account surplus—foreign investment in the Keynesian sense.

And how do you increase investment? You depreciate the real exchange rate. That creates or increases a current-account surplus, and thus creates or increases foreign investment. You therefore have less need to attract capital funds, so you reduce the rate of interest. That increases your domestic investment, and, as your domestic investment and your foreign investment increase, you need less stimulus to consumption, and so can raise taxes. You end up with a balanced budget, with that degree of investment which is necessary for a balanced budget, and with a distribution between home investment and foreign investment which the market determines.

*Kaldor*: May I just ask one more question, and then I'll shut up. Your targets are a stable value of money—in the specific sense in which we discussed this—plus a rate of growth of income, in money terms, that would be consistent with this stable value of money. To get your desired growth of income, an autonomous element of demand must grow. Now where do you look for that? Do you look for it in home or foreign investment? Or do you look for it in a growing budget deficit?

*Meade*: Well, I've just explained. If you find you've got to do it by a budget deficit—and don't want to—you make the changes I have indicated, which will get the stimulus out of private investment. I don't think there is any problem there.

*Matthes*: It seems to me, Professor Meade, that your proposal implies a complete departure from what, to my mind, has been a recent achievement of monetary policy—namely, the shift to what monetary policy can really attain, which is control over the volume of money. Your concept implies a new intermediate aim—or, rather, the return to an old intermediate aim; you want the central bank to control the interest rate and the exchange rate, both in real terms. The central bank would then be burdened with all the old difficulties of making this into a workable monetary policy, and we would be back to the 1960s and 1970s, when central bank policy was very difficult indeed.

*Mundell*: The Meade proposals seem to me to be geared to solving certain problems peculiar to the trade unions in Great Britain. Meade has provided us with a good analysis of what probably happens with the T.U.C. in Britain when that country approaches full employment. At such a time, the trade unions strike for very high wage settlements, because, as Meade points out, they're interested in maximizing the incomes of the employed, not the labor force as a whole; their clientele is the *employed* labor force.

But surely the important thing is to change the conditions under which the unions have so much monopoly power. I would say that if anyone wants to form a union with a collection of workers who insist on getting $150 an hour, or whatever, let them go ahead and do it. But don't let them impose that wage rate on nonunion members or on other people in the working community who want to work for wages that are closer to reality. And one shouldn't assume that the monopolistic power held by trade unions in Britain is characteristic of other countries. India doesn't have that problem. The United States doesn't have that kind of thing; the trade unions represent only 15 or 20 percent of the U.S. labor force. Canada doesn't have that problem, and many other countries don't. So don't impose it on the rest of the world.

But as a sometime resident—and as a friend—of Britain, I would not recommend James Meade's scheme to the British. Instead, I would recommend that the British government peg the pound sterling to the dollar at a rate of somewhere around $1.50, and let that be the monetary policy of the United Kingdom. Period. Nothing more. The unions could set wage rates anywhere they wanted. But with a stable exchange rate (including, if needed, a stabilized forward rate), interest rates would stabilize and come down, and the British would achieve a far higher level of employment and a lower rate of inflation than they have had at any time since the floating-rate system began back in 1973.

*Gutowski*: Just a sentence or two. I think we can all agree that, in one way or another, discipline in the labor market has to be imposed; it has to come from somewhere, and I agree with Professor

Meade that the wage-settlement problem is *the* central problem, not only for Britain, but for Germany, France, other European countries, and elsewhere. This is not just an isolated British problem.

*Kaldor*: Mr. Chairman, I want to say that, as between James Meade and Bob Mundell, I'm on the side of James. And my understanding, which may be very imperfect, is that the Meade proposal, though in somewhat new garb, is very much in the tradition of early postwar British policy as laid down in the famous White Paper of 1946. This is not surprising, because James Meade was one of the principal authors of that White Paper. And I entirely agree with Professor Gutowski that the success of holding wages down, one way or another, is the key to the success of the full-employment policy. If you succeed in that, the rest is relatively easy; if you don't succeed in that, the rest just won't work.

As far as full employment is concerned, we have known all along, at least in Britain, that there are two ways of maintaining it. We can have a relatively high-consumption, low-investment economy, or we can have the reverse. Under the postwar Labor government, we operated a high-investment, low-consumption economy; it used to be called "Crippsian" austerity, after Sir Stafford Cripps, the chancellor of the Exchequer. And it induced one of our great economists, Sir Roy Harrod, to his one important lapse. He wrote a book in the late 1940s entitled *Are These Hardships Necessary?* Well, they damned well *were* necessary, but Harrod's book may have contributed to the Tory cry that we needed to cheer up the country and to have full employment, by all means, but with more consumption and less investment. So the investment plans were sharply cut by the succeeding Tory government under Mr. Butler in 1951. That, combined with rearmament, led to troubles for a long future.

I don't want to go into all that, but it's pretty clear that it is an inferior thing to rely on a budget deficit to maintain full employment. Because what are you doing? You are saying, "This country is oversaving relative to its investment at home and abroad." Therefore, you cancel this alleged oversaving through a cut in taxes that makes the disposable income of consumers larger than it would be under a balanced budget. I think I am entirely on the side of Sir Stafford Cripps and of James Meade—that the preferable way to have full employment is to have high investment. That requires a balanced budget or even a budget surplus, but certainly not a large budget deficit.

Now you can achieve this the best way by what I call the Japanese policy. It's very simple. The Japanese put the rate of interest low, and keep it there, irrespective of what happens—a very different policy from that pursued by Mr. Volcker. Whereas the rest of the world follows the American rate of interest in such a way as to maintain exchange relativities, the Japanese follow the opposite policy; they maintain a low rate of interest, and allow the exchange rate to fall to the extent necessary to make up for the loss of interest resulting from the undervaluation of the yen. The advantage of this is that, at a low rate of interest, you have more home investment, and you may also have more foreign investment in the form of a current-account surplus.

And the Japanese prefer it that way. Their output will be composed more of the dynamic industries which have a future and less of the consumption-goods industries which don't have a dynamic future. So I think the Japanese are doing things jolly right. And they have succeeded in Professor Gutowski's main condition of keeping money wages down. They do this, not by the Meade way, but by the opposite way—by the way which the Germans, the Austrians, and any other countries which are successful do it, and that is by centralized wage negotiations and centralized wage control.

I am in favor of a statutory, not a voluntary, incomes policy, and I am in favor of a centralized, not a decentralized, one. I favor a centralized policy to avoid the tendency, which is particularly strong in Britain, to what is sometimes called "leapfrogging." The most important thing about wage bargaining is relativities.

*Cooper*: Is what?

*Kaldor*: Relativities. I can cite any amount of evidence that workers don't care nearly as much about the absolute amount of the real wage as about how their wages are related to the wages of workers in other activities. What happens in a wage round in England—it goes on all the year—could be avoided if, as a former Labor government proposed, all these negotiations were simultaneous and not spread out over time. If they're spread over the whole year, as they are in England, then there develops a going wage rate. That going rate is always excessive, and terrible troubles happen if any particular class of workers gets less than the going rate. Well, that argues very much against decentralized wage controls; they build an inflationary bias into the whole system.

This is the part of the Meade Plan which was least well spelled out. I think that, in a country like Britain, you must have compulsion in wage negotiations. You might get by without compulsion in Germany because of the terrible experiences that Germany has gone through. The Germans are terrified of inflation because of their experience with hyperinflation; they can listen to reason. So when the central bank tells them, in a somewhat concealed way, that wages must not rise by more than 7 percent—by announcing that a 7 percent increase in the money supply is the only one consistent with a stable price level—they recognize that if they demand more than 7 percent, they frustrate the objective of price stability. In England, you would also need a body that deals with anomalies—what I call an "anomalies commission"—which sees to it that wages here and there can be adjusted if they depart from normal, historically hallowed relativities. The difference in wages between a bricklayer and his mate is a hallowed relativity; according to our economic historians, it hasn't changed, percentagewise, for the last five hundred years. And we have lots of examples like that. But there are relativities which people accept as fair and others which they consider completely unfair. The feeling of unfairness is the most important driving force behind excessive wage increases.

So the success of the Meade Plan would depend on an incomes policy that has to be statutory and that has to provide in an organized way for a correction of anomalies. The policy should include a monetary commission which monitors the whole thing and sees to it that the regulations are really obeyed. But, given that, I'm all in favor of Crippsian full-employment policies which go in for high investment, therefore low interest rates, therefore low exchange rates, as against the policies which other British governments have followed—of high interest rates, low investment, high consumption, and a steady deterioration of our situation, both from the point of view of productivity growth and from the point of view of our share in the world market. In Britain, the direction has been down, down, down. This would not have happened if the policy of Crippsian austerity had been maintained after 1951.

*Scharrer*: Only a very brief comment on Germany. I would agree with Lord Kaldor that the centralized process of wage bargaining in Germany has major advantages, but I'm a bit doubtful whether it is possible to apply this example to other countries. My second point is that, whereas on the whole this process has worked well, one can see certain problems in the recent past, as compared, for instance, with the United States, where it has been possible to negotiate wage reductions—both nominal and real wage reductions—for firms which were in economic trouble and where both employers and employees agreed that by additional wage restraint the firms might be rescued. This does not work in Germany.

*Kaldor*: Your unemployment is not so high.

*Scharrer*: Well, it's high enough.

*Kaldor*: But what if the employer says to the workers, "Either you agree to a wage reduction or I have to shut up shop, liquidate the business, and declare bankruptcy"?

*Scharrer*: Even in that case, it is impossible to negotiate a wage reduction at the level of the firm, as the wages negotiated for an industry must not be undercut by individual firms. The wages negotiated for the industry are, in effect, minimum legal wages.

*Gutowski*: What Lord Kaldor said could easily trigger off another discussion of several hours or so, but I will be brief. The main thing I want to say is that the German wage-negotiation system has proved to be much less satisfactory than many people think it is. We Germans haven't given enough attention to the structure of real wages and to qualitative differences, with the result that low-quality labor has been priced out of the market. In Japan, the situation is somewhat different, because that country has a rather flexible system. I don't want to go into details, but the subject is perhaps important enough to be the theme of another conference.

*Triffin*: I merely want to say that we shouldn't forget the success of Austrian incomes policy.

*Kaldor*: And we shouldn't forget Norway.

*Gutowski*: Let's talk about that in two years.

*Cooper*: I would just make one remark about Lord Kaldor's reference to Japan. I think that before we extol the Japanese too much, either as a model for others or even as a model for Japan in the future, we ought to look at the role that swings in the external balance have played in maintaining full employment in that country. Japan, although it had a fixed exchange rate for many years, was able to manipulate its external balance, partly through aggregate demand manipulation while staying on a more or less steady growth-of-capacity path. And that is something which a country with a small economy can do without much impact on the rest of the world. But Japan is now the second largest economy in the world, and one of the difficulties that the Japanese are having is shifting the emphasis from external demand management to internal demand management. Singapore can do what Japan did in the 1950s and 1960s, but Japan cannot do in the 1980s what Japan did in the 1950s.

*Scharrer*: I would like to look at the Meade scheme against the background of an already existing scheme—namely, the European Monetary System. Leaving out certain details, I would interpret the Meade Plan as a sort of improved or more elastic EMS.

Now what has been the experience with the EMS? The experience has been that, despite numerous consultations and coordination processes at various levels, inflation rates within the European Community have persisted at high figures, and have continued to diverge among the three largest countries within the regionally pegged exchange-rate arrangement—namely, France, Germany, and Italy. If you look at the EMS over the past four years since it was created, you come up with the result that, over the period as a whole, the occasional exchange-rate changes that have taken place have largely accommodated the inflation differentials.

*Kaldor*: And have reinforced them too.

*Scharrer*: Well, okay; that's another question. But the process by which this has been done has been cumbersome, and has meant that interest rates have been highly volatile, especially in the two or three months before a realignment of exchange rates within the EMS has taken place.

These observations apply to maintaining real exchange rates. But a rule which says that you should attempt to keep real exchange rates stable, while perhaps appropriate in a regional setting, may perhaps not be sustainable in a global setting, given the external shocks that may call for changes in real exchange rates in order to bring about real adjustment. So, as Professor Meade has pointed out, there may be occasions when you wish to change the real exchange rate. And there, I think, you get into the Bretton Woods type of problems which the chairman mentioned earlier. How you incorporate changes in real exchange rates without destroying the credibility of the system, I don't know.

*Vaubel*: I would like to supplement Dr. Scharrer's observations about the European Monetary System. I think the experience with the EMS has taught two very clear lessons, neither of which is a matter of theoretical necessity but rather a matter of brute fact.

The first lesson is that an adjustable-peg system like the EMS leads to increasing restrictions on international capital movements. The outstanding case is France over the last year, but there are other cases. On the other hand, you have the case of the United Kingdom, which is not a member of the EMS exchange-rate arrangement, but which, significantly, is the only member of the European Community that has abolished such restrictions. This experience leads me to doubt whether one can really say that the European Monetary System has contributed to more economic integration within Europe.

The second very clear lesson, I believe, is that as long as monetary and fiscal policy are as divergent as they are in the European Community and in the OECD, an adjustable-peg system like the EMS makes it impossible for individual member countries to follow a steady and preannounced monetary policy. The outstanding example

over the last few months is Germany. From the beginning of this
year to the parity adjustment, there were foreign-exchange interven-
tions in the EMS leading to an increase of German central bank
money—the German monetary base—of DM 16 billion, or between
9 and 10 percent of the total. In addition, there was an exchange-rate
induced cut in the discount rate that will also lead to an increase in
central bank money. As a result, the German monetary base is far off
target, and it's very doubtful that it will get back into the target band
by the end of the year.

What this means is that the public at large no longer has a pre-
announcement on which it can rely. Since there are two targets—a
monetary target and an exchange-rate target—and since monetary decisions are made on a case-by-case basis, the public has no way of
knowing what monetary policy the Bundesbank will pursue. I think
that these two brute facts would emerge on a much larger scale if the
EMS were to serve as a model for international monetary reform for
the West as a whole.

*Mundell*: I agree with Mr. Vaubel that the EMS is not a good
model for the world economy. It couldn't be, because it's a fixed exchange-rate system within a much broader floating-rate system—
within a floating-rate system in which the level of international reserves of each of the countries in that system is subject to vast and
violent fluctuations.

*Matthes*: Just to correct Dr. Vaubel, it was not an increase in
central bank money but an increase in central bank reserves—a fundamental difference. Moreover, those DM 16-17 billion have already
left Germany—indeed, the outflow has been greater than the inflow—so, seen from this perspective, the earlier inward movement
need not worry us at all.

*Vaubel*: Well, I entirely disagree with that, because I believe that
credibility of the steadiness of monetary policy does matter; I believe
that it does matter whether monetary expansion is steady from
quarter to quarter or not.

*Cooper*: Howard, do you want to say something on that?

*Craven*: Yes; the increased uncertainty arises from the dual
goals. The question I have in mind is whether this uncertainty is a
plus or a minus with respect to the impact of monetary policy. The
matter is viewed differently in different countries.

*Cooper*: I have a question which is a variant of Howard Craven's
question. When Vaubel made the assertion that steady quarter-to-
quarter increases in the monetary supply are necessary for steady expectations about I'm not sure what—that's my question: What is it

necessary for? In the U.S. case, for example, three quarters of central bank reserves are in the form of currency. Currency growth has been behaving in a very funny way in recent years; currency has been growing very rapidly even when interest rates have been very high and when one would expect the demand for currency to go down, not up. Now if the United States, like Germany, were to have a central bank reserve target, this would mean that higher than normal growth of currency would have to be offset by lower than normal growth of member bank reserves, which would put a tremendous squeeze on the credit system. And I'm just wondering—without getting into a discussion of monetarism in all its forms—what is the world that makes the steady quarter-to-quarter growth of this particular measure of money so important for stability of expectations? It seems to me that you can easily cook up examples in which it creates uncertainty, rather than certainty, for the business world. That's a question; one might call it a rhetorical question.

*Vaubel*: You have mentioned one possibility, but even if you deny the negative credibility effect, which I don't, then you have the fact that, in the deviant quarter, you get an excess supply of money; that changes the demand for goods, and destabilizes output.

*Cooper*: But if it is known, as was evidently the case in the EMS, that there will be a temporary inflow of funds before, and an outflow of funds after, a realignment of currencies—that's the standard pattern—why should this influence business behavior in any way other than speculating against the central bank during the period of adjustment?

*Vaubel*: Well, in many cases money doesn't just flow in and out again. The experience in Germany has often been a persistent deviation from our monetary targets; 1978 was a marvelous example.

*Matthes*: Most of the funds which then flowed in—DM 16 or 17 billion—went into the banks, and didn't enter into the German money supply at all. On balance, we even had a negative effect on nonbank liquidity positions, so one need not worry at all about that. I don't mean to say that one should not be concerned about deviations from monetary targets—but not for the reasons that preoccupy Dr. Vaubel.

*Kaldor*: So, in Germany, foreign-owned balances are not counted as part of the money supply?

*Matthes*: It depends on whether they are held by banks or by nonbanks.

*Kaldor*: If they are held by banks, they are not regarded as money?

*Matthes*: No. It is in the discretionary power of the Bundesbank to introduce compensating measures, which we did; we cut the discount quotas. It is of course a long transmission way from an influence on the liquidity position of a bank toward lending, toward deposits, and so on. There is a multiplier which is derived from that, but everything depends on whether the central bank becomes active or not.

*Meade*: May I make one comment on an earlier statement? I've kept quiet on a very ridiculous criticism of my proposals by Bob Mundell. This raised a big laugh, and I wasn't sure whether the laugh was at his nonsense or at me; I am therefore very anxious to see that the right person is laughed at. How on earth any reasonable man . . .

*Cooper* [*interrupting*]: There's your error right there.

*Meade* [*repeating*]: How on earth any reasonable man—much less an extremely intelligent pupil of mine—could say that I have tried to impose the British T.U.C. wage-fixing system on the world; well, it beats all.

*Cooper*: Didn't you mean an adaptation of the T.U.C. system?

*Meade*: No, no—no adaptation. I said that as far as the international system is concerned, I think it would be better for countries to have nominal GDP as their monetary target; that, as far as their home arrangements are concerned, they should be absolutely free to decide whether they distribute that among employment or unemployment, or whether they have centralized wage-fixing arrangements, whether they have trade unions, whether they have anything they like. How on earth this can be put forward as making people step in line with the U.K. in some way, I simply can't understand.

*Mundell*: You didn't say monetary target in your earlier presentation; you said financial policies—policies to manipulate aggregate demand in such a way that the nominal growth of GDP is 5 percent, or $X$ percent, adapted for other countries. Now, in my understanding, every country wants that as a particular goal, but that's not an instrument. The problem has always been how to achieve this goal. You haven't said how monetary and fiscal policies are to be adapted in order to achieve this objective.

*Meade*: I thought I had.

*Mundell*: Now if you say that you want to do that for the world economy; you want the world economy to grow in nominal terms by 5 percent or $X$ percent—we won't quibble over the figure—then our objective should be to try to find monetary or fiscal policies in each country which will achieve that.

*Meade*: I must have been misunderstood; one country can choose zero percent, another country can choose 5 percent, another country can choose 10 percent.

*Mundell*: Agreed; no problem.

*Meade*: I'm allowing countries to decide what suits themselves. And then I'm saying, "How can we build this into an international system that will work when people have very different wage-fixing arrangements, very different targets for growth of nominal national income? How can we build what I will call a new Bretton Woods that takes this into account?" But how can that be interpreted as chaining every country to what suits the U.K.?

*Mundell*: No, you had five proposals, and these proposals, it seemed to me, were to counter the grave distortions you described in the British economy.

*Meade*: Well, what I said was that I wanted to get rid of these problems.

*Cooper*: Max looks as though he might clarify this.

*Corden*: I'll try. First, I would like to say that when Bob Mundell made his earlier remarks, I was one of those who laughed. And I said to myself that Bob ought to respect his elders and betters! But let me attempt a few words of clarification. From an international perspective, the Meade proposal boils down, as I understand it, to a monetary policy for external balance—that is to say, a monetary policy aimed at an exchange-rate objective. In a world of perfect capital mobility, it implies nonsterilized intervention, so the interest rate actually becomes endogenous. You decide on the exchange rate, and that is the bit where James says there has to be international coordination. I don't think there necessarily has to be, but it's one possibility. Then he proposes a policy of internal balance, meaning a nominal GDP growth achieved by fiscal policy. So we have one particular Mundellian set of assignments, which can be restated in terms of Bob's own work. The third element is the question of how to get to full employment. That's where James became very British and mournful and dispirited, because things always look worse in Britain than they do in wonderful countries like Austria and Norway.

That's my short-run analysis, leaving aside the longer-term implications. Is this essentially, James, a correct interpretation?

*Meade*: Yes, I think so.

*Mundell*: I surely should be able to make a comment.

*Cooper*: Brief?

*Mundell*: I'll be brief. I accept the idea—it's a good one—that our goal should be a nominal GDP growing at a rate of, say, 5 percent. As a condition for that, money growth is probably going to have to be something like 5 percent, modified by the income elasticity of demand for money and by variations in velocity over the short run. Of course, you might end up with nominal GDP growth of 5 percent and inflation of 8 percent, which would mean real growth of minus 3 percent; that would be terrible. In order to cope with that problem, you would have to let unemployment discipline the wage rate, as the monetarists would have it; or you would have to have some kind of incomes policy; or you would have to remove the monopoly power of the unions, which set wage rates in excess of productivity and which impose the burden of their actions on the unemployed.

*Meade*: Yes, absolutely.

*Mundell*: That's the way I see the problem. But Meade's domestic objectives are best accomplished within the framework of an international monetary system rather than in 151 or so national monetary systems operating under floating exchange rates. We should try to work toward a monetary system of the kind we had for the Western economies under Bretton Woods or, for the world economy, under the earlier metallic standards.

Now you can't have a fixed exchange-rate system operating successfully while international reserves are subject to gross and unpredictable fluctuations. And since the price of gold is the principal element determining the instability of international reserves at their market value, the approach that we should take is to stabilize the dollar price of gold. The European Monetary System may fit into that picture in one way or another, but the fact is that there is no common government within the EMS that can produce a separate EMS currency. But a currency almost as important as the complex of currencies that enter into the EMS is the dollar. The dollar has played the role of a global currency for the past forty or fifty years, and it probably will be the most important international currency, by far, for another forty or fifty years. Why not make use of the fact that we are to a large extent a dollar-oriented world? That means, as the secretary of the Treasury said last week, that the United States can't intervene in the exchange market the way that other countries intervene. But other countries can do what they did under Bretton Woods; they can peg their currencies within agreed margins to the dollar or, indirectly to the dollar, through the EMS.

We should not impose a Volcker standard on the world economy, but there should be some arrangement that makes the dollar a stable international currency. And that arrangement, as I see it, would restore the convertibility of the dollar into gold, as under Bretton

Woods. All this involves is to reimpose Article IV 4(b) of the IMF Articles of Agreement, and establish a dollar price for gold of, say, $350 or $400 for another thirty years or so. Then we'll have to have another conference. But that's not too bad.

*Matthes*: I just want to express my skepticism about magic rules. We all know that the Bretton Woods system didn't work. And why didn't it work? Because it degenerated into a hegemonic system, dominated by the United States.

*Mundell*: No, no, that isn't why it didn't work. It didn't work because, with gold priced at $35 an ounce and with Americans prohibited from holding gold, the system couldn't survive after three major wars.

*Jamison*: I would like to change the subject and make some long-range comments of a much more general nature.

In the 1930s, the world experienced depression, both economic and psychological. Not only was there a low level of economic activity, but there was also a gloomy conviction that the world has reached economic maturity, that the era of substantial growth was over—and over permanently. At the other extreme, in the 1960s there was an era of optimism and euphoria, when at least some economists believed that we had entered an age of strong, sustained, and permanent expansion. With "fine tuning" we had reached the millennium, and even recessions were a thing of the past.

How wrong they all were! In recent years, the pendulum has swung back in the other direction. It appears that we have sunk into a state of mind somewhat reminiscent of the Great Depression. There is a widespread belief in severe limitations on growth. There is an obsession with the limited nature of natural resources. Fears are widely expressed that there are no driving forces left to raise the world economy into a new growth era.

I believe that these feelings are unduly pessimistic. Not that there isn't a surplus of economic problems; there certainly is. Recessions undoubtedly will continue to plague us from time to time, and sooner or later we may even experience another major depression with a capital *D*. But somewhere down the road is a new era of dynamic growth, abundant energy resources, and substantial improvement in real income. And at that time our successors will look back and wonder why we were so strangely negative in our thinking back in the 1980s. End of comment.

*Cooper*: Thank you very much for that optimistic note.

*Heller*: Mr. Jamison has just given us a great vision of the future. The question is: How do we get there?

I think the first thing we should work on is a new agreement in the area of international trade to facilitate structural changes in the world economy and to ease the adjustment process. Two things are in order here. First, we should eliminate all subsidies; if we cannot eliminate them immediately, we should at least work in the direction of reduction. Then, for the countries that do eliminate subsidies, there should be a reciprocal agreement that gives those countries totally free access to each other's markets. Among other benefits, that will help prevent excessive wage increases, because British steel workers, to take one example, will be facing Korean steel workers.

On the international monetary side, a central issue, raised by Mr. Vaubel, relates to freedom of international capital movements. Clearly, the Bretton Woods system was not designed for free capital movements, and that's why, in my view, the system broke down. If we want to have such freedom, I don't see any alternative to flexible—at least movable—exchange rates. If we're willing to forgo freedom of capital movements, then we can have fixed exchange rates.

*Kaldor*: It took a hell of a long time for the Bretton Woods system to break down.

*Heller*: Well, the story wasn't all that happy either.

*Cooper*: The system wasn't in effect for the first fifteen years of its existence; that's worth keeping in mind too. Max has the floor.

*Corden*: Because it's getting late, I was going to forgo my comments and say that I have some very profound and important remarks to make, and that anybody who wants to read them should send me a self-addressed envelope and $20. But there still may be time to offer them here.

*Cooper*: Well, it's 5:30, but I think we should give you time.

*Corden*: I want to get away from Bretton Woods and all that; may I?

*Cooper*: Certainly.

*Corden*: Sometimes at a conference, someone says something that strikes a chord; you say, "I've been thinking that for a long time, but neither I nor others have articulated it; there must be something to it." I'm thinking of the comment made by Mr. Jamison that things are not as bad as they seem. And I ask myself whether, in retrospect, we aren't in future years going to feel that we were looking at this period in history in an excessively pessimistic way. Incidentally, in Adam Smith's *Wealth of Nations*, there's no reference to the Industrial Revolution, is there? Apparently, Smith didn't see it on the horizon.

*Kaldor*: It started twenty years later.

*Corden*: I mean he didn't see the first signs. It may very well be that, in retrospect, we will find that we are living now in a new Industrial Revolution—this fantastic computer and microchip revolution—with all the wonderful developments that are coming from Japan and elsewhere. And this new revolution is going to have a very significant impact on the world's standard of living.

Now, I think, we shouldn't ignore this. The issue of protectionism is relevant here, because there seems to be considerable resistance to accepting some of the implications of these major developments. It's too late, obviously, to think or talk about this at any length here, but I wish to draw attention to it, partly because our measures of economic growth may not fully include these benefits. I haven't thought this through, but I suspect they can't. And this may be one reason why recorded growth in recent years has been so small.

*Cooper*: Any comments?

*Gutowski*: Yes. What Max appears to be saying is that if we have an improvement—a big increase—in productivity, then this would ease all our economic problems. I would agree if, and only if, we solve the problem of the distribution of income and wealth. This is a central problem. It would be easier to solve if we have increases in productivity; nobody would deny that, but there still would be the question of how the income, or potential income, from this increase in productivity would be distributed—both inside the countries where it occurs and internationally. I don't believe that we shall be able to avoid serious technological unemployment unless we really learn how to distribute income and wealth without impeding growth. And this is a matter for long discussion—a question of how to convince people that they will be better off if distribution is not totally equal, or of how to bribe them by a certain kind of redistribution in order to make them comply with a viable system.

*Kaldor*: Doesn't this micro-whatnot revolution automatically imply a huge growth in productivity? It can't help it. In other words, it is nothing less than a revolution in the amount of output attributable to one worker; if the worker has all his robots and microchips at his side, he will produce that much more.

*Gutowski*: May I respond to that? This *is* technological progress; whether it's labor-saving or capital-saving or both, we can have more output with the same amount of resources. And, if we don't want that, we can have fewer labor hours. Either way would improve wealth, but the question of distribution still remains.

*Heller*: Wouldn't the GNP actually fall if we suddenly have all these marvelous things?

*Cooper*: No, no, no.

*Heller*: No? We're doing all these marvelous things; what used to take $1,000 to produce we can now do for 50 cents. We may be producing twice as much as we did before, but our measure of nominal GNP is down.

*Corden*: What I had in mind is what we're seeing now and on the immediate horizon—so many improvements in the standard of living.

*Cooper*: Right.

*Corden*: For example, the opportunity to multiply TV channels.

*Heller*: But this is not caught in the GNP statistics.

*Cooper*: That was Max's point.

*Corden*: That's right, that's my point. But I don't think that these developments reduce GNP; I'm not suggesting that, though the increase may not be fully caught. I'm wondering, for example, whether the word-processor revolution, the office-equipment revolution, and so on, are fully caught, since so much of this goes into the public sector. Do we catch that in the public-sector productivity measures? I'm not sure.

*Cooper*: We have no public-sector productivity measures. Outputs are measured by inputs, and to the extent that employment goes down in the public sector—which is not a worry in most people's minds—GNP would actually fall.

*Kaldor*: But surely there is a problem here. With all these wonderful new inventions, we may have a situation in which the real earnings of those in employment go up very much, whereas the number of people employed goes down very much. That would be the worst kind of situation from a social point of view.

*Cooper*: That's the distributional point.

*Craven*: Perhaps this discussion can be summed up in the statement that the central problem of the twenty-first century will be how to make constructive use of increased leisure time.

Richard N. Cooper

# Concluding Reflections and a Radical Blueprint

Let me begin by saying that I will *not* try to summarize our discussion during the past two days. I do, however, want to make one set of observations on this morning's dialogue on the recovery, and an observation—or, rather, a proposal—having to do with the long-run nature of the system.

My first observation on this morning's discussion is one of surprise that, as I detected it, there was less of a sense of urgency about the world recovery than I, at any rate, think there should be. I infer that everyone thinks world recovery would be a good thing. There was not, however, anywhere close to agreement that any action should be taken to bring it about, and among those who thought such actions might be taken, there was disagreement about what the actions should be. Sometimes, the prescriptions even went in opposite directions—for example, as to whether the United States should raise or reduce taxes. But I would like to remind you of the point that Lord Kaldor made—that there are always a thousand reasons, at any moment in time, for not doing anything and that the costs of a prolongation of the present world economic situation are exceedingly high. And they are not measured merely by the unemployment which we now have—although I don't denigrate that—but in all the major countries, though not in the poorer countries of the world, we have found systems which cushion the economic cost to those who are unemployed.

Let me mention some of the things which, as we look at the trade-offs between action and inaction, we should keep in mind. One is that lost output implies lost investment. We're going to be paying for this recession a decade from now in lower capital stock. And that lost investment is huge. The United States alone, one can reckon, is forgoing about $300 billion a year in output, and if one were to add Europe and Japan, the figure would be almost twice that—probably half a trillion or more a year. Suppose that 20 percent of this is investment; that means that the capital stock of these countries, taken as a group, is at least $100 billion per annum lower than would otherwise be the case. So we pay a long-run price, not just a short-run price, for this.

Secondly, there is the alienation of youth.

*Kaldor*: That's an important point.

*Cooper*: This, I think, is a grave risk—that young people put years into training of some kind, and, for reasons not having to do with their own qualities, find themselves, month after month after month, pounding the streets looking for a job. Even though they may not be suffering from an economic point of view, the result is self-doubt, loss of self-respect, and, I fear, alienation from society. And that's happening in all of our countries.

We talked about the external debt problem. The countries with debt problems, with weak terms of trade, with poor export markets, are being put under an enormous squeeze to pay for these debts. It is in a sense remarkable that, so far, they have continued to do it—some, to be sure, with arrears—but if this were to go on much longer, the point is going to come, I fear, when political opposition to current governments is going to make hay out of it. New groups may come into power and repudiate that debt, and that would then trigger a whole series of events, including events in the trade area, to isolate such countries—not to mention fast stepping by the central banks to prevent reverberations throughout the banking system.

But that's not what I want to emphasize; I do actually think that this part of the problem is manageable. It's the political instability that should worry us. In our countries, it takes the form of changing governments, but we should keep in mind that in most countries of the world it takes the form of changing systems; those countries don't have the constitutional framework that the democracies do. I think we are in serious risk of losing the liberal trading system if this goes on. With the possible exception of the French government—and even that has held the line so far—there's no doubt that all of the political leaders of the major countries are committed to maintaining the liberal trading system: Mrs. Thatcher, Mr. Reagan, and so forth. The question is whether they can continue to do it under the pressures that are increasingly put on them—whether they'll find the whole thing eroded from under them. And if the erosion is extensive, it will take a decade to restore the situation as it existed, say, in 1980. So, again, there's a long-run cost.

And, finally, it's precisely in these circumstances that the government role in national economies goes up, both in the form of transfers to ease the economic burdens on the unemployed and in the form of control of, and subventions to, the firms that otherwise would go under. It's a paradox that one of the inhibitions in all of our countries is the concern today about the size of government; the result of this inhibition to further action may well be more, not less, government intervention in the economy as a result of the prolongation of these kinds of economic circumstances.

But the solution for which we're all reaching, as I detect it, is to knock on wood, cross our fingers, and hope that world recovery will prevent all these things from happening. I find that attitude—perhaps being more activist than some of you—a sad and regrettable state of affairs. And I do think that much more is at issue here than the simple movement along the Phillips Curve that Max Corden drew our attention to—rightly, in my opinion. This is a *deliberate* recession. Although the parameters may not all have been guessed correctly, this is exactly where the Federal Reserve has wanted to drive us, with cheering on by similar bodies in other countries. The central bankers may have moved us further than they wanted to go, but they did so, I fear, without taking these other factors into account. Thus my short-run pessimism.

Abstracting now from the world recession and moving to the longer-range issues—and it would take much more time than I should allow myself to develop this theme in any length—I think that the path we're on, given the technological imperatives that I see coming along, is not a sustainable one. The technological imperatives are basically a continuation of the process which has already been taking place over the last two or three decades, but, with the electronic revolution which has been alluded to, it's going to continue at a pace at least as great. Essentially, the process reduces frictions; the world becomes much smaller for purposes of communication, for purposes of trade, and so forth. Foreignness goes out of foreign transactions, and the barriers of ignorance and lack of information that tend to insulate national economies are diminishing very rapidly. And the frictions which we have relied on, to a greater extent than I think we are aware of, are gradually disappearing. That is going to put tremendous pressure on our ways of doing things, including framing national economic policy.

There are two possible reactions to that. One is to rebuild the frictions as a matter of policy. Protection, after all, is a reaction of this kind, and, in a curious way, the move to flexible exchange rates was a modest move in the same direction. Like James Meade, I don't like this trend, and what I'm now about to propose makes Meade's proposal look practical and operational by comparison. My proposal is not politically feasible now, but I'm trying to project a twenty-five-year horizon, and ask what kind of world we might be thinking about moving toward in the domain of international monetary relations—certainly not next year, not in the decade of the 1980s, but perhaps a quarter of a century from now.

Both Vaubel and Heller, rightly in my view, concluded that freedom of capital movements is incompatible with fixed exchange rates—I interpret them to mean *adjustable* fixed exchange rates—and therefore we need exchange-rate flexibility. There is a more radical solution to that problem—one which Bob Mundell has been pushing toward, although with the curiously archaic feature of having gold in it. This seems to me not only unnecessary but unbelievable—incredible in the sense that you don't get the mileage that Bob wants by linking to gold, because learning is irreversible, and we've learned that we don't need gold.

My radical solution would be to move to one currency. Without going into all the details, what I can envisage by the year 2005 or 2010 among the industrial countries—let's think of the OECD; I'll come later to the rest of the world—is a free-trade zone in which all tariff and nontariff barriers are permanently eliminated by agreement and in which there is a single currency. That, of course, raises the question of what that currency is and how it is governed. Like Mundell, I think the natural candidate is the dollar. There are some psychological hang-ups with that, I recognize, elsewhere in the world. But, from a rational point of view, it seems to me that the hang-ups are irrational if the management of the currency is suitably internationalized. And therefore the key to the one money is not what it's called or what it is but how it's managed.

Here, I think, we need a single central bank. One might think of using the Federal Reserve System as a model, because, after all, when the United States adopted a central bank, it was quite a decentralized country. From an economic point of view, the world has fewer frictions today—more centralization—than the United States did in 1913 when the twelve Federal Reserve districts were set up. So one can think of a central bank among the industrial countries in which policy decisions are made by an open-market committee consisting of national governments which sit as national governments—and they all vote. They would have weighted votes; I would use GNP for the weights, but the decisions would be made collectively. The open-market committee, through its collective decision-making, could then target whatever it wanted to target: any of the Ms, to which I personally would be opposed, or nominal GDP (we'd have to call it GRP—gross regional product—to cover the collectivity of member nations), or, as I would prefer, and think in the end would be inevitable, the monetary policy could be discretionary, with nominal GRP, the Ms, interest rates, and perhaps other economic variables serving as indicators. But that debate won't cease whether you have national central banks, a world central bank, or something in between.

And here's the James Meade part of it. Under these conditions, fiscal policy becomes terribly important; it becomes the principal national macroeconomic policy. Fiscal policy in these circumstances, however, cannot count on financing by the regional central bank; countries would get their share of new money from the normal open-market operations—that is, from normal monetary expansion—neither more nor less. They would have to go into the capital market to finance budget deficits, so there would be a natural inhibition on wild fiscal policy. But with the kind of capital market that I envisage under this system—and toward which we're moving anyway—there would be freedom for member countries to go to this market to finance budget deficits or to retire government securities if that's what they wanted to do.

So fiscal policy would be the principal national macroeconomic policy. I say nothing here about incomes policy; that could also be done at the national level if people chose, but although, like Lord Kaldor and James Meade, I think the attempt should be made, I'm rather pessimistic about success. I think that success, however, would be more likely to be achieved in this regime—a regime totally without trade barriers—because of the competition from other countries within the region. Such competition would be the principal discipline against national wage movements that were out of line.

I'm driven to this proposal partly because I think that flexible exchange rates in the last several years have been one of the sources of uncertainty that inhibit foreign investment. I have to be careful about how I put this; I don't want to attach the primary blame to flexible exchange rates—after all, exchange-rate fluctuations reflect mainly the divergences in national economic policies. But they are also the transmission mechanism of these divergences to the entrepreneur who has to make business decisions. In the United States, we don't feel this quite so much, although we feel it much more, I think, than is believed by most American economists, who are still fundamentally closed-economy in their thinking. But in an open economy, movements of the real exchange rate of the order of 5 or 10 percent surely must give pause to any investor who is making a fine calculation about laying out capital investment which will mature in two to five years, unless he is very sure of a high rate of return.

So I see the movement to one currency and one monetary policy as a way of forcing harmonization of at least one important dimension of national economic policy and of putting constraints on the other dimensions of national economic policy—but not of straitjacketing them to the point at which they can't serve a useful stabilization function. Of course this proposal is not close to being negotiable at the present time, but it seems to me that it is the kind of regime we should be thinking about for twenty five years from now. And if we find it either repugnant or completely unattainable, we'd better be thinking very seriously about optimal frictions to put back into the system, because I think that the present system is just not going to endure with the reduction in national frictions, provided by distance and ignorance, which we've relied on up to now.

*Kaldor*: May I ask two questions on what you have just said? First, are you convinced that, if your system were realized, not only would world real income be higher than under any other system, but also that the real income of each particular continent, each particular country, and each particular distinguishable region would be higher than under a system which does not have a common currency and which has trade barriers? Secondly, do you envisage that the inequality between the rich countries and the poor countries under your system would be greater or less than it is now?

*Cooper*: On the first point, I am in no position to compare this system with all alternative systems, all possible conceivable systems. But I am convinced that real income would not only be higher, but substantially higher, than under what I see as the likely alternative system, which is protectionism.

*Heller*: For the world as a whole?

*Cooper*: Well, for this group of countries; I'm going to come back to the world as a whole. For this group of countries, I do see that real income would be substantially higher than I think are the now likely alternatives to this kind of system. Now the question is whether that observation translates into higher real income for each and every area of this larger region. The answer to that is: not necessarily; the possibilities are there, but the assurance is not there—just as the assurance is not there today within nations or between nations. But larger regional real income at least creates the possibility of having a larger real income within each subregion.

Let me now say more about the membership of this group. I would have it open-ended in its membership, but I would start with the European Community, the United States, Japan, Canada, and those smaller European countries which felt that it was consistent with their foreign policy to join such a group. That would be the core, and I would essentially operate laissez faire with respect to the other countries of the world. I would suspect that, following Mundellian reasoning, many of them would choose to tie their currencies to the region's currency, but they certainly would not be obliged to; they would maintain the freedom that they now have to pursue independent monetary policies, independent exchange-rate policies, and independent commercial policies.

*Kaldor*: You appear to rule out the possibility that the joint income of the whole group of countries could be lower under this system of free trade, laissez faire, and a single currency than under a system of regulated trade which provides a higher total volume of employment and a better utilization of resources than is consistent with free trade.

*Cooper*: I do not want to state an existence theorem that the system I have proposed provides a higher real income than all conceivable systems; I do want to state a likelihood theorem that it provides a higher real income than all likely systems, including systems that begin to interfere with trade under the name of providing employment and, in fact, screw themselves up—which is what's likely to happen under such regimes. So it's really a likelihood proposition, not an existence proposition. Well, I just throw this out as something to mull over for the future.

*Corden*: If we have twenty five years to think about it, perhaps this subject could be discussed two years from now at our next conference.

*Kaldor*: I propose that Professor Cooper spend a couple of years at Cambridge University, not as a teacher and not as a pupil, but as someone with whom to discuss these matters.

# Name Index

# Subject Index

Randall Hinshaw is professor emeritus of economics at the Claremont Graduate School. He is the editor of several volumes, including *Monetary Reform and the Price of Gold: Alternative Approaches, The Economics of International Adjustment,* and *Inflation as a Global Problem* (all published by Johns Hopkins).

*The Johns Hopkins University Press*

**World Recovery without Inflation?**

This book was composed in
Trump Medieval and Helvetica
Black display type by EPS Group,
Inc., from a design by Martha
Farlow. It was printed on 50-lb.
Glatfelter B-31 paper and bound
in Holliston Roxite A with Cela-
don Multicolor endpapers by
Thomson-Shore, Inc.